The Last Jacobites

The Last Jacobites

Heroes, History and Culture after the Battle of Culloden

Keith Coleman

PEN & SWORD
HISTORY

First published in Great Britain in 2024 by
Pen & Sword History
An imprint of Pen & Sword Books Limited
Yorkshire – Philadelphia

ISBN 978 1 39904 562 9

A CIP catalogue record for this book is
available from the British Library

Typeset by Mac Style
Printed in the UK by CPI Group (UK) Ltd, Croydon, CR0 4YY.

MIX
Paper | Supporting responsible forestry
FSC® C013604

Pen & Sword Books Limited incorporates the imprints of After the Battle, Atlas, Archaeology, Aviation, Discovery, Family History, Fiction, History, Maritime, Military, Military Classics, Politics, Select, Transport, True Crime, Air World, Frontline Publishing, Leo Cooper, Remember When, Seaforth Publishing, The Praetorian Press, Wharncliffe Local History, Wharncliffe Transport, Wharncliffe True Crime and White Owl.

For a complete list of Pen & Sword titles please contact

PEN & SWORD BOOKS LIMITED
47 Church Street, Barnsley, South Yorkshire, S70 2AS, England
E-mail: enquiries@pen-and-sword.co.uk
Website: www.pen-and-sword.co.uk
or
PEN AND SWORD BOOKS
1950 Lawrence Rd, Havertown, PA 19083, USA
E-mail: uspen-and-sword@casematepublishers.com
Website: www.penandswordbooks.com

For Agnes Skelly and Allan Skelly

And Chairlie o' the gowden heid
Won little support till he was deid

Hugh MacDiarmid,
'To Circumjack Cencrastus' (1930)

Contents

Author's Note

In this work I have given the heads of the exiled Jacobite house of Stuart a variety of names, in accordance with the titles and nicknames they were known as in their lifetimes and afterwards. I hope this will not cause confusion. James Francis Stuart, may well have been known as James VIII and III by his loyalists, but he was also known as the Old Pretender and other things to those who opposed him. Charles, his son, was called Charles III, Bonnie Prince Charlie, plus a variety of unflattering alternatives. The first Jacobite, James VII and II, retains his royal titles in the text, even though he was deposed and fled abroad. The last in the royal line was Henry, Cardinal Duke of York, hardly ever called Henry IX.

List of Illustrations

Introduction

For most people the story of the Jacobites ended on a dour April morning in 1746, when their aim of restoring the Stuart monarchy withered forever in the blood-soaked moorland. Survivors fled from the Scottish battlefield of Culloden into hiding or exile; prisoners were taken south and many faced execution or transportation. The Stuarts had lost the British throne half a century before and the dream of restoring it may have continued in the minds of some supporters after that day, but most who had fought for the cause naturally looked to their own survival. Just over sixty years later the last legitimate male descendant of the dispossessed royal house died in Italy and the remote hope of restoration that he still embodied evaporated. A few may have mourned the last remnants of the deposed dynasty, but there was no remaining political Jacobite movement.

Yet the Jacobite vision lingered on. Beyond the allure of the 1745 Jacobite rebellion and the campaign and romantic flight of Bonnie Prince Charlie, heroically evading the British enemy after his defeat and then fleeing to France, there are other people's stories. And when the last adherents of the exiled Stuarts died themselves, Jacobitism persisted in several forms, down to the present day. It survived as a romantic echo, a historical disaffection, a symbolic adherence, a nod to the divine right of kings, a Scottish obsession, a direct line to some imagined, more noble past. It means many things to many different people. There may even have been a few people who watched the pomp and spectacle of the coronation of King Charles III in 2023 who could not easily accept that royal designation. Shouldn't there have been another King Charles III once, British also, but from an entirely different royal family? And if that eighteenth-century Stuart Charles was the rightful king, what does that make our present monarch?

Leaving that treacherous thought aside, we should begin by asking what a Jacobite was in the beginning. At the most fundamental level, the Jacobites were a motley group of supporters of the royal house of Stuart, who lost the throne of Great Britain in 1688 and never got it back, though various armed attempts and plots sought to accomplish this for the next century. In 1660, King Charles II had returned triumphantly from exile to England after a period of fraught exile in Europe. His father, Charles I, had been executed and the nation entered an austere period of republican rule. The golden age of the Restoration ended with Charles II's death in 1685 and the assumption of the throne by his rather less capable brother, who became King James II of England and VII of Scotland.

For all his talents as a military man and administrator, and there is ample evidence of both, and willingness to consider wider religious liberty, he was rigid in authority and incapable of instilling widespread loyalty in his subjects. His unflinching Catholicism in an overwhelmingly Protestant nation rang alarm bells with many important religious and political figures, not least the Whig faction, who became long-term enemies of his house. A rebellion by the Duke of Monmouth, a natural son of his brother, was put down, as was another in Scotland by the Duke of Argyll. But the momentum for his downfall grew and, after three short years of rule, his son-in-law (and nephew) William of Orange invaded England.

Instead of organising a proper defence with his superior military resources, the king's nerve soon broke and he fled overseas. A subsequent landing and campaign in Ireland was mismanaged, and so he was sent back to France forever, where he died in 1701. As head of the exiled royal house, James II became the first Jacobite, a term for the movement espousing the royal Stuart cause, derived from his name. Many Britons, whether they were ready to bear arms or not, could not countenance that the throne was in the hands of foreign usurpers.

Both James II and his son, another James, easily disprove the myth that the royal Stuarts were a charismatic, enchanted lineage. Their adherence to the divine rights of kings was ironic in light of their own shortcomings, even if their loyalty to the Roman Catholic religion spawned another subsidiary regal Stuart legend, which survives to this day: the idea that this ruling family was in some way saintly. The deaths of Mary, Queen of Scots in 1587 and her grandson Charles I in 1649 were thought of as being martyrdoms by some adherents. The Stuarts had long believed they were God's anointed rulers and would hardly brook any contradiction to this conviction. This concept of divinity, together with the stubborn Catholicism of King James II and his successors, meant that they were viewed as unacceptable to rule in Britain. But the aura of divinity was fostered and retained by the royal Stuart dynasty. One example of this is the Stuarts' continued fondness for curing sufferers of scrofula, a type of tuberculosis also called 'king's evil', which had been the prerogative or monarchs to cure since the Middle Ages. Before the fall of the Stuarts, King Charles II touched so many of his subjects who hoped to be cured of this painful condition (possibly around 105,000) that it has been wondered whether there was something miraculous in the fact that he did not succumb to the infections eagerly brought to him by his subjects. One of the royal successors to the Stuarts, William of Orange, cynically carried on the practice and was heard to comment to one supplicant as he laid on the magical touch, 'God grant you better health and more sense.'

Both Pretenders and the last royal Stuart, Henry, Duke of York, continued the practice. But the German Hanoverians, the cumbersome royal family that ultimately succeeded to the British throne, had no time for such nonsense. One subject who went to George I and requested the royal touch to cure his malady was bluffly told that, if he wanted such a service, he should resort overseas to the court of the Stuart Pretender. The supplicant took him at his word and went to visit the 'king over the water' in Italy for the royal touch and remained a committed Jacobite ever afterwards. The first three Hanoverian king Georges ruled from 1714 to 1820, and their reigns saw the defeat of the most serious Jacobite uprisings and, by the end, they happily outlived the last direct descendant of the old line of kings.

Yet, for a while, it seemed that the Stuarts would only be temporarily absent on the continent. James II had been displaced by a man who married his daughter, Mary. Another daughter, Anne, afterwards became queen. It also seemed like a family disagreement that would perhaps be settled amicably one day. James II died in 1701 in France, disappointed, but true to his ideals and strongly held faith. Calls for his canonisation several decades later came to nothing. The exiled king's son, James Francis Edward Stuart, was known by his enemies in Great Britain as the Old Pretender. As well as a crumbling claim to the thrones of England, Scotland and Ireland, James inherited his father's pessimistic nature and largely gave up practically trying to regain his birthright following the 1715 uprising in Scotland, during which he had played an uninspiring part. There was an opportunity for James to succeed his half-sister Queen Anne and triumphantly return to his homeland, but it would never happen, for he would not renounce his religion. During Anne's reign England and Scotland became politically united as Great Britain and those Scottish Jacobites who supported the Stuarts had another grievance that threw them into the arms of the deposed dynasty which had its origins in Scotland. Many thousands of people in Great Britain supported or at least favoured the exiled Stuarts in preference to the Hanoverian dynasty that followed Anne in 1714. Not least, the Tory party, which contained a sizeable number of Jacobites, could never quite muster the energy, courage or resources in England to stage a Stuart coup and second Restoration. Many sympathisers in England (and some elsewhere) were happy to be passive Jacobites but would never openly commit to the cause. They were habitually 'Hanoverian when sober, Jacobite when drunk'. True, local mobs occasionally chanted slogans and vocalised support for the deposed line of kings at riots, fairs or elections, but rarely did it do more than express rebellious discontent. Jacobite drinking and social clubs survived the political side of Jacobitism and survived in a pallid form in some places into the nineteenth century.

For a further thirty years after 1715, the prospect of the Stuarts returning from the dynastic grave of exile to rule their old nations again was a very real prospect. In Scotland, Ireland, England and Wales, in exiled groups in France and Italy and elsewhere, these followers plotted and planned and hoped for the return of the rightful ruling house, but it did not happen, and the dream ended disastrously at the end of the '45 uprising. In the century from the overthrow of King James II to the death of his grandson Charles Edward (later styled Bonnie Prince Charlie by nostalgists), the family had repeated opportunities to reclaim their royal birthright. But continued poor judgement and bad luck ensured they remained as one of history's collective greatest losers. It could be said that the Stuarts were enormously fortunate when they came back into power after exile once; very few dynasties manage to be kicked out of their home nations twice and then make two successful comebacks.

The event that elevated the Jacobite claim from a minor sideshow in the politics of major European powers was the campaign waged in 1745–46 by James Edward's son, Prince Charles Edward Stuart. With minimal backing from France, he landed in Scotland and drew a large army to his cause through his determination and bravery. During the uprising he attempted to do the impossible and win back the crown for the Stuarts, persuading some wavering Highland chiefs (albeit not enough of them) to the Jacobite cause by his personal magnetism. His personality was an ingredient in drawing people to his cause. One Scot counselled another indecisive friend about his uncanny charm, and perhaps incidentally coined his byname, which became popular in the following century. To him, Charles was almost uncanny, 'ye Bonny Prince…who if he once sets eyes on you will make you do whatever he pleases, therefore do not see him'. Even after the defeat at Culloden, his adventures in avoiding the search parties of British soldiers in the Highlands for two months drew admiration throughout Europe. In Scotland and later in Europe, where he was adept at evading Hanoverian spies, he took on a trickster-like persona. While it lasted, his charisma was seen as a resurrection of one of the best qualities for which the royal Stuart family was renowned, until it was dissolved in alcohol and his character degenerated.

Jacobitism, despite determined efforts by its supporters, withered away as a political force well before the end of the eighteenth century. Yet some consciousness of the Jacobites crept back during the early part of the nineteenth century, part of a cultural resurrection of Celtic nostalgia, arising from the ashes of Highland Scottish Gaelic culture that had been severely damaged for supporting the royal Stuarts. Jacobitism ironically became a fascination for the new monarchy, the Hanoverians, and in a sense, they had the ultimate victory in being integrated into British royal identity by Queen Victoria and her successors.

From the late Victorian age onward, the influence of the movement could still be felt in many circles. One strand of Scottish nationalism had its roots in allegiance to the Stuarts and still smarted at the decimation that their defeat at Culloden had imposed on their nation. Others in the modern age redefined Jacobitism within a wider adherence to the house of Stuart, stretching it back to an interest in the dynasty that included kings Charles I and II and linked in with the concept of kingship as a divine prerogative which was sadly lost when the Hanoverian kings succeeded to the throne.

The aura around the defeated royal dynasty lingers strangely. There is a persistent myth that the royal Stuarts were a particularly ill-fated race. Louis XVI of France (who was beheaded in 1793) believed that the Anglo-Scottish Stuarts possessed the evil eye and loftily declared, 'The Stuarts are an unlucky family; I wish to hear no more of them.' The Old Pretender himself seemed to credit this myth that his lineage was cursed. According to his adherent Charles Wogan, James was a character 'whom a continuous chain of misfortunes and reversals since birth had already made over-pensive and over-serious'. Even followers of the cause sometimes wondered whether the family was ill-omened, probably because of its own actions. An Irishman named Macnamara who got into an argument with the Young Pretender in 1755 rhetorically asked him, 'What has your family done, Sir, to draw down the vengeance of heaven on every branch of it through so many ages?' The truth of the dynasty's fortune is rather different, if judged in terms of its longevity in power. The Stewarts/Stuarts ruled Scotland for 232 years before becoming kings of Great Britain for a further 111 years. Added together, this span can be favourably compared with the similarly long-lived Plantagenet dynasty, which ruled England for 331 years. By most reckonings, the Stuarts had a good run for their money and should have left the royal stage graciously.

Although the Jacobites had capable supporters, there were multiple instances of the royal leaders of the party and their adherents being incompetent, weak or indecisive when it came to taking positive steps to reclaim the throne. The Bishop of Rochester, Francis Atterbury, was behind a plot in 1721 to restore the Stuarts. But he was severely compromised and eventually defeated by the incompetent Jacobite hierarchy and lukewarm co-conspirators. 'Never was a better cause lost for want of spirit,' he commented with disgust, which is an adequate epitaph for the whole Jacobite century, 1688–1788.

On the other hand, it is easy to fall prey to the belief that the Stuarts overall possessed a glamour and mystique that was conspicuously absent in the royal house which displaced them. The first Hanoverian rulers, George I and George II (who ruled 1714–60), were unpleasant individuals and all too human kings. The last Stuarts, for all their failings, were mostly a better lot. James II, the Old Pretender and Cardinal Henry of York were not overwhelmingly despotic or evil, which is not to say they would have made better kings than their German replacements. Bonnie Prince Charlie, on the other hand, became a wife-beating alcoholic who abused all and sundry loyal to him in the end.

Scotland, the chosen battleground for the civil war between British royal houses, had not wholeheartedly followed the Jacobite uprisings of 1715, 1719 and 1745. Those who did support the Stuarts' right to re-establish their kingship were swayed by loyalty to the old native ruling house and by the commitment of the Stuarts to reverse the Act of Union of 1707, which shackled Scotland to England and formed the political state of Great Britain. Ever since, Jacobitish has been entwined, sometimes uncomfortably, with Scottish identity.

Jacobites in Ireland, unlike Scotland, followed the 'rightful' Stuart king after his overthrow in 1688 for religious reasons and many successive Jacobites through the years since have associated the shadow royal house with Catholicism, closely linked to the divine right of kings. And yet, as Ireland struggled towards its own national independence from Britain, it quickly divorced itself from attachment to the house of Stuart. Towards the end of the eighteenth century the political landscape seemed very different to the romantic royalist enterprise that characterised Jacobite aspirations. Radical uprising in France as well as the establishment of the American republic re-mapped the world order. In Britain, meanwhile, the establishment seemed to be reversing into the future while looking longingly at some aspects of the past. The most extraordinary example of this was the visit of King George IV to Edinburgh in 1822, where he made an eye-watering appearance bedecked in a fantasy tartan version of a Highland chieftain. Jacobite and Gaelic culture were reclaimed by the establishment and subsumed within the greater British identity. The visit to rehabilitate recently rebellious Scotland was partly engineered by the writer Walter Scott, whose genius soon propelled a romantic vision of the nation throughout the western world. Scott and contemporaries like James Hogg (as well as later Scots like Robert Louis Stevenson) created a more nuanced and ambivalent view of the recent Jacobite past, which was soon swelled by the production of sentimental, yearning Jacobite songs and literature throughout the Victorian period. In the nineteenth century too there sprung up individuals and new groups dedicated to the lost cause of Jacobitism. Among these were Pretenders such as the Sobieski brothers, who claimed descent from Bonnie Prince Charlie and launched the spuriously authentic industry of tartan into the world.

Despite the fact that there was negligible realistic chance that descendants from the house of Stuart would replace the Hanoverians as the rulers of the United Kingdom, there were individuals and societies who promoted this ideal through the late nineteenth and into the twentieth century. This was despite the fact that the 'Jacobite succession', which passed through the noble house of Savoy and other aristocratic continental dynasties, was ever more remote from any connection with Britain. The putative heirs to the Jacobite succession themselves never claimed the right to the British throne, and in some cases seemed embarrassed that such a dubious birthright had been imposed upon them. The First World War ensured that these mostly German claimants were never again seen as politically viable alternative royals in Great Britain. Together with those who could legitimately claim to be offspring from the side branches of the royal Stuart family tree, there have been others whose claims have either been dubious or outright fraudulent, and the fact that these shadow pretenders have expended so much energy and will into their charades gives us reason to consider the strange allure and legacy of the Jacobite movement, which survives to the present day.

Yet the concepts and cultural force of Jacobitism continued into the modern age. This was evident in the continuing stream of books, music and films inspired by the Jacobite uprisings and their aftermath, most recently the *Outlander* series of books and TV series, which have highlighted the events of Scottish Jacobite history. The political and philosophical sides of Jacobitism linger also via commentators on the internet and small groups that seek to promote and preserve their own concepts of the movement, whether connected to Catholicism, the divinity of kings, or other more recondite ideals. The fact that such groups exist, arguably more successfully than others devoted to other historical movements, gives cause to consider why the Jacobites have survived in the popular imagination. Part of the appeal is undoubtedly the sweep and romance of the 1745 rebellion that sought to restore the Stuarts. Those men who participated in the doomed campaign were lionised by some for decades after the failure. But there are other stories too, of men and women who negotiated perilous adventures following the Battle of Culloden and ensured that the ideals they fought for were not entirely lost. Some of their tales are contained in the pages of this book, which seeks to give them their proper place in the fascinating story of the latter-day Jacobites.

The heroes of Jacobite legends are a fascinating and disparate assembly of men, devoted in various degrees to the deposed royal family and usually paying a significant price for their loyalty. None of them was recognised as an untarnished leader or participant in the tumult of their own times and all their reputations are tangled up in divisive judgements of them and their actions. Even before the final Stuart fall from royal grace, the dynasty had its dazzling champions. The proto-Jacobite champion was James Graham, 1st Marquis of Montrose, who conducted a mercurial military campaign across Scotland in support of the embattled King Charles I and ended up on the gallows in 1650. Soldier, statesman, poet and possible martyr, Montrose outraged the staunch Presbyterian Covenanters when he switched sides to become an avowed supporter of the king. Even more controversial was Montrose's kinsman, John Graham of Claverhouse, Viscount Dundee. An ardent persecutor of Covenanters in south-west Scotland, Claverhouse had many extraordinary attributes attached to him by friend and foe alike. He rose in the wake of the fall of King James VII of Scotland and in opposition to William and Mary in 1689 and displayed military genius in his campaign across the Highlands, becoming the first true Jacobite military hero. To his religious enemies he was a full-fledged vassal of Satan, nicknamed 'Bloody Clavers'. To supporters (or was it only to romantic songsmiths long after his death) he was 'Bonnie Dundee'. The Gaels whom he led gave him the admiring appellation 'Dark John of the Battles'. Dundee snatched death from the jaws of victory, succumbing to a random musket shot while leading his Jacobite forces to victory against the Hanoverians at the Battle of Killiecrankie in 1689. It was said by some that he could only be slain by a silver bullet and it was otherwise rumoured that, after his death, he was found to be wearing the surcoat the Knights Templar, a fittingly ambivalent and mysterious military-religious order. Dundee was also more lauded after his death than he was in life, something that can also be said of other Jacobite figureheads. The nobility of Scotland conspicuously avoided following him into battle, though the tide of support in the nation turned again in the rebellion of 1715, when there was great support for the Stuart cause. Gordon of Glenbucket despairingly called upon the spirit of the dead hero at the Battle of Sheriffmuir in 1715: 'Oh, for one hour of Dundee!' But Graham did not come back from the dead to save the day.

In the second tier of those who fought in the Jacobite cause are ever more ambivalent figures whose designation as heroes might be viewed as highly contentious. High-profile members of the aristocracy like Simon, Lord Lovat, signed up for the Stuart cause, while sometimes courting the opposing British establishment. Cunning and cynical though he was, Lovat eventually reconciled himself to defeat and died bravely on the executioner's block. More shadowy characters among the ranks include Alan Breck Stuart, one of the main characters in Robert Louis Stevenson's *Kidnapped*, a figure linked to international Jacobite intrigue and connected by some to the notorious post-Culloden murder of the government official Colin Campbell, known as the Red Fox. Others were not so clear cut in their loyalties since their lives reflected the complicated political and social currents of eighteenth-century Britain. In this group were Dr Archibald Cameron, a reluctant volunteer for the Jacobite cause, and Flora McDonald, who famously conspired with the Young Pretender to aid his escape after defeat, but later became an Empire Loyalist in North America.

Chapter 1

The Royal Stuarts

It is appropriate that the origins of the royal house of Stewart, later called the Stuarts, is mired in mystery and the supernatural. The first of the house to rule in England was James I (VI of Scotland), who likely listened to Shakepeare's play *Macbeth*, which included an approving (and unhistorical) nod to his own supposed ancestor. In the play, the king's companion Banquo is a minor character who is told by the trio of witches that his descendants will be king. Banquo's son Fleance was recognised as a founding figure of the Stewarts. Genius though he was, Shakespeare's historical research extended back no further than Ralph Holinshed's late-sixteenth-century *Chronicles of England, Scotland, and Ireland*, and Holinshed himself filched the material from the florid Scottish historian Hector Boece, who wrote at the start of that century. Boece wrote that Fleance married a daughter of a Prince of Wales and they had a son named Walter FitzAlan, who migrated to Scotland and became the steward of the king of Scots. Walter was certainly a real person, but the historicity of Banquo and Fleance are dubious.

The first traceable member of the Stuart family was a Breton warlord named Flaad, who entered English service under King Henry I, together with his son Alan, at the beginning of the twelfth century. Alan's son Walter migrated to Scotland and became *dapifer* or steward in the household of King David I, also serving the following two monarchs. The role became hereditary in the family, who became notably powerful magnates in the west of Scotland. The Stewarts, as they became known, became the royal dynasty of Scotland when the male line of Robert Bruce failed in the fourteenth century. Robert Stewart, son of Walter the High Stewart of Scotland, married Bruce's daughter Marjorie and became king of Scots in 1371. The next nine monarchs of Scotland were Stewarts, including King James VI, who inherited the throne of England in 1603.

As to the argument that this Scottish royal house was exceptionally ill-fated during their tenure holding the throne, it seems convincing at first glance. King James I was ignominiously murdered in the sewer of a monastery. Nearly as embarrassing was James II's demise: he was blown up by his own malfunctioning artillery. King James III was stabbed by an assassin while blundering around after being defeated in battle by his son. That son, James IV, died bravely but needlessly in the front rank of his army at the Battle of Flodden. Mary, Queen of Scots, of course had her head removed by her cousin, Elizabeth of England. As dark as that catalogue seems, it is arguably no worse than the fates of some other European royal houses during their tenure in power.

The doomed glamour of the house only began to be acknowledged during the tumultuous life of Mary, whose woeful personal choices, combined with being the victim of repeated hapless misfortune, created a dramatic lifespan. She also possessed that mysterious quality of glamour that some have associated with the whole house of Stuart. The most fascinating of the Scottish monarchs was that queen's grandfather, James IV, who combined personal magnetism with a broad intelligence and interest in the affairs of his kingdom and wider world, which was unmatched by any of his royal relatives, and his untimely death in war against England, along with thousands of his countrymen of all degrees, added a dark lustre to his legend.

Mary's son James VI succeeded through a combination of guile, intelligence and undeserved good luck in succeeding Elizabeth. It was James, flushed by his success, who encouraged the concept of the divine right of kings as embodied in his own person. This most intelligent but mundane ruler entirely failed to recognise the irony that this concept was in marked contrast to his own capabilities and, to be fair, he did not invent the idea and nor was he the first European king to promote it. The house of Stuart did not learn sufficient lessons after the degradation of Charles I's death. The collective groan that ran seismically through the crowd which witnessed his beheading said more about English conservatism than any deep attachment to their ruling house. Charles II, it is true, read the mood of his nation by loosening the societal strictures that were imposed upon the country by Oliver Cromwell, the Commonwealth and the Puritan party. But in retrospect the decadence of the Restoration was a last, hedonistic hurrah for the Stuart dynasty. The descent of the crown from Charles II to his brother James (II of England and VII of Scotland) heralded the end of the ruling male line of the Stuart dynasty. James II, for all his arguable virtues, was an unlikely figure to inspire the complex, alluring cult of Jacobitism. Despite his staunch Catholicism – which cost him his crown – James was more widely admired before he actually became king. He was an active and brave military officer in the French army (and later served Spain) during his early exile in Europe following his father's death. The contrast between the young military hero who prided himself on his decisiveness and the king whose indecision led to his own defeat, is marked. His own fall from the throne had its comedic as well as tragic elements. Fleeing precipitously from his enemies, he dropped the Great Seal of England into the Thames, symbolically making the point that, if he could not be king then nobody could. Even this he could not accomplish properly. The seal was retrieved by some fishermen in a million to one chance, no doubt greatly astonished at their catch.

After he lost his throne, James sunk into defeated exile on the continent, a miserable legacy that was bestowed on his son, James Francis Stewart, known as the Old Pretender. Another characteristic that he seems to have bestowed on his unfortunate descendants was his inability to sustain the promise of his own youth. James II had fought an extended but unsuccessful campaign against his successor William III in Ireland, 1689–91, and then never troubled British or Irish shores again. The Old Pretender landed in Scotland too late to make any meaningful contribution to the 1715 Jacobite uprising. Despite a sizeable following among the lords and lairds of Scotland, the rebellion ran out of impetus and could not capitalise on gains made in the north of Scotland. The Battle of Sheriffmuir, on 13 November 1715, was a stalemate and a thrust into England was defeated at Preston.

Many Stuart followers were unimpressed by the prime leader of the campaign, John Erskine, Earl of Mar, and the equally uninspiring James Francis Stuart. James Francis did not land in Scotland until December 1715, by which time the impetus of the uprising had been lost and he did little to bolster his followers. The rebellion in 1719 was more promising in having international allies in Spain and Sweden, but ill fortune in the death of the Swedish monarch Charles XII meant that the coordinated invasion of Britain was stillborn and the small Spanish and Jacobite exile force that landed in the north of Scotland was easily mopped up. James Francis played no active part in this effort. He lived until 1766 but had no active interest in regaining his throne during the rest of his life.

Early promise and mature atrophy were the fatal weakness that was either passed down or cruelly bestowed by fate upon the last royal Jacobite hopeful, Prince Charles Edward Stuart, James II's grandson. By some dark coincidence, this last true heir to the throne of the Stuarts died on 30 January 1788, the anniversary of the execution of his great-grandfather King Charles I.

Chapter 2

The Aftermath of Culloden

Culloden, the last battle fought on native soil, was a peculiarly drab event even by British standards. This final military encounter between the Hanoverians and Jacobites, fought on 16 April 1746, was also a short and brutal battle, less than an hour long, shorn of any glorious military incidents, though it spawned a contrarily momentous place in legend. The actual aftermath too was particularly appalling for Highland Scotland, with bloody reprisals against those who were deemed to have supported the Jacobite insurrection and harsh laws imposed against Highland dress and the hereditary rights of leaders, which led to a steep erosion in the clan system and Gaelic culture.

The final Jacobite military campaign began when Charles Edward Stuart, tired of both the defeatism of his father and cynical French intransigence in promising support for his family's cause, attempted to seize his own destiny. In summer 1745, behind the backs of the Old Pretender and the French, he commissioned a ship and set sail for what he regarded as his native realm on 23 July, arriving on the island of Eriskay. The story of the whole fourteen-month Jacobite odyssey known as the '45 has been told and retold many times in many ways: in sober chronological terms, in the frame of military history, as a false bookend event in the long-standing struggle between England and Scotland, and not the least as a sorrowful romance.

Raising the support of a number of clans and others (though not enough), the Jacobites captured Edinburgh and much of Scotland, then advanced into England as far as Derby. The opportunity to press on towards London was spurned because of dissension in the senior ranks, with Irish and Scottish leaders in opposition. It might have been different if the French had invaded and opened up a second front in England to support their Jacobite allies. A further reason to withdraw was that large numbers of Highland irregular troops, the backbone of the Jacobite army, were demoralised. Traditionally these troops had been called upon for short local campaigns and so they did now what they had done before: withdrew from the fighting and returned home in December 1746.

The Jacobite army also turned north to Scotland and inevitably fell back into the fastnesses on the north of Scotland. Its successes during the remaining months of the campaign were negligible. The burgh of Stirling, for example, fell to them after a siege at the beginning of January, but it was meaningless because the strategically crucial castle in the town remained in government hands. The Battle of Falkirk, fought on 17 January 1746, was claimed as a Jacobite victory (and it would be the last) despite most of their forces abandoning the battlefield. The Duke of Cumberland brought substantial government forces north and began to pursue the Jacobites. If not absolutely caught in a noose, the odds began stacking against the Jacobite army. The Lowlands were controlled by the government and no further help could be gained from overseas as the Royal Navy was effectively patrolling the Scottish coastline. The Jacobites took Inverness and captured Fort Augustus, but other military targets including Blair Castle and Fort William resisted them. In the middle of April, the Jacobites failed in their attempt to surprise government forces during a raid at Nairn. The Battle of Culloden was fought two days later. The two sides, led by princes Charles Edward and William Augustus, Duke of Cumberland, met on the sodden moor of Drummossie at Culloden on a dank spring day.

The Jacobite army was unpaid and some segments of it was demoralised; resources were also running low. Many of their men were also deployed elsewhere, in Badenoch, Fort William, or in Sutherland keeping an eye on government forces under the control of the Earl of Loudon. Some estimates reckon that as many as 2,000 men, between a third and a half of available soldiers, were not present in the Jacobite ranks at Culloden. Their army comprised around 4,000 men, facing 9,000 troops of the British army. Cumberland's army advanced to meet their opponents on a sparse section of moorland not far from the house of that ardent, though humane supporter of the government, Duncan Forbes of Culloden. The ensuing encounter was won by the government through a combination of factors. One was the superiority of tactics; they had learned how to drill and defend against the onslaught of the Highland charge following earlier encounters. Their weaponry was also superior to that of the Jacobite army and, when the fighting started, they successfully goaded the enemy into an early charge through the use of artillery, then cut many of them down. Many of the Jacobites on the left flank got bogged down in the waterlogged terrain and were neutralised. The scene quickly degenerated into a one-sided killing field, during which the Jacobites lost around 1,500 men, which was thirty times as many as suffered by the government army. The whole event may only have lasted forty minutes.

The battle, and the campaign, was a domestic conflict, though not between Scotland and England. The Jacobite army contained Highland and Lowland Scots, but also Irish, English, French, and several other nationalities. Many of the clans who had been traditionally loyal to the Stuart cause had conspicuously boycotted participation, understandably reluctant to commit to an ad hoc rebellion that was ill-planned and woefully under-resourced. One clansman, unconvinced of Prince Charles's credentials, bluntly told him on their first encounter that he should return home. 'I am home,' the prince retorted. But his bravado still did not outweigh the huge risk that he was asking Highland Scotland to undertake on his behalf. Some chiefs therefore prevented their followers from bearing arms for the Jacobite army. Other communities were divided and some landed families carefully sent one son to support the insurgents while another safeguarded their interests by maintaining loyalty to the state.

The majority of Scotland supported the Whig establishment and the Hanoverian crown, though the balance of actual support on either side is debatable. Many burgh authorities supported the Stuart monarchy, and large communities of non-juring Episcopalians who refused to accept the new kings were strong in the north and north-east of Scotland (alongside Highland Catholics who had the same loyalties). Weighed against the Jacobites, the English establishment's primary weapons were the indolence of the Jacobite-favouring Tories, plus the indifference and blind loyalty of the majority of the population.

Immediately following the battle, the victorious British troops pursued the enemy soldiers, killing hundreds who were trying to flee. Many who tried to head for Inverness were easily caught on the roads and slaughtered. Elsewhere there were still substantial groups of Jacobites at liberty. Clan leader Cluny Macpherson gathered his own men together with survivors of the right flank of the army, some 400 men in total, and rested at Loch Moy. The commander Lord George Murray had 1,500 men with him, though most of them were suffering from acute hunger. He led these to Ruthven barracks and joined others. Most of the commanders there expressed willingness to continue the armed struggle. The prince thought otherwise and sent orders for his forces to disperse, advising them, 'Let every man seek his own safety as best he can.' This last brief message was conveyed to the men by Lord George Murray and Lord John Drummond. James Johnstone, who would soon escape to France and write an account of the campaign, *Memoirs of the Rebellion in 1745 and 1746*, memorably captured the dejection of the defeated Jacobite survivors at Ruthven:

> We bade one another an eternal adieu. No one could tell whether the scaffold would not be his fate. The Highlanders gave vent to their grief in wild howlings and lamentations; the tears flowed down their cheeks when they thought that their country was now at the discretion of the Duke of Cumberland, and on the point of being plundered; whilst they and their children would be reduced to slavery, and plunged, without resource into a state of remediless distress.

There was no realistic option to reassemble a sufficiently large Jacobite force that could be mustered quickly enough to tackle the British forces in the Highlands. Besides which, there was no great store of food to feed them, and they were poorly armed and unpaid. Surviving Jacobite combatants had the unenviable choices of surrender, going into hiding locally, or attempting to escape abroad into exile, if they had the money and connections to do so. Charles Edward may have hoped his loyal men could regroup in the near future once expected aid came from France, but no such event occurred.

The aftermath of Culloden had a strange effect on the characters of some of the participants. Simon Fraser, the aged Lord Lovat, who had spent a sly lifetime weighing up the odds of Hanoverian and Jacobites, and acting in his own best interests, had decided during the campaign to at last declare for the Stuarts. He was too old to do any fighting or lead men into the fray, but he had a vast store of intelligence and influence that may have served the would-be prince regent if they had met earlier. They did not encounter each other until after Culloden, when Lovat tried to reassure the prince: 'Remember your great ancestor, Robert Bruce, who lost eleven battles and won Scotland by the twelfth.' But his advice to stay and fight on was not followed. Another nobleman who remonstrated with the prince was David Wemyss, Lord Elcho, a Lowland nobleman who had first served abroad under the Old Pretender before returning to Scotland and intriguing with other upper-class Jacobite sympathisers. When the uprising began, he wished, like many others, that the young prince would swiftly return to Europe, for what hope was an armed uprising without a very substantial force of French troops to back it up? He may have been influenced by the opinion of Lord Sinclair, a Jacobite veteran of the '15, who advised him to take the side of the Hanoverian regime in London, sagely observing that the Stuarts were an ungrateful race. They regarded everything done for them as simply the fulfilment of duty. It would be madness, he said, to risk life and fortune for such a weak dynasty.

As the Jacobite army proceeded south out of the Highlands, however, Elcho had a change of heart and met Charles Edward outside Edinburgh, bringing with him a gratefully received contribution of £1,500 for the cause. He was close to the prince through most of the remainder of the campaign and commanded a troop of cavalry, though he strongly opposed the retreat from Derby in December 1745. Following the Battle of Culloden, Elcho actually managed to escape to France before the beleaguered Young Pretender reached the safety of that nation. In France, he was shunned by other Jacobite exiles for purportedly offering his allegiance to the Hanoverian cause. But he served in the French army and later migrated for a while to Switzerland, returning later to France where he died in 1787.

Elcho's fame, or notoriety, in Jacobite circles was sealed by his manifestly acerbic views of Jacobitism, captured in his work *A Short Account of the Affairs of Scotland, 1745–1746*, which did not appear in print until 1907.

He was more famous for one of the most furious put-downs in history, which allegedly occurred in the cold light of defeat at the Battle of Culloden itself. Seeing Prince Charles Edward fleeing precipitously from the field of conflict, David Wemyss furiously berated him as 'an Italian coward and a scoundrel', which later retellings altered to, 'There you go for a damned, cowardly Italian!'

Did Elcho actually utter any such words? Different accounts of clashes between the men were given by Sir Walter Scott in his journal entry on 10 February 1826, and a later article in the *Quarterly Review*. His anecdote has Elcho in the closing act of the battle informing his royal highness that all was lost and nothing remained to do other than charge at the head of 2,000 men who were still unbroken. They would either turn the tide of the battle or die honourably with swords in their hands. The prince mumbled evasively, then turned his horse and rode silently away from the field. The infuriated nobleman sent him on his way with his damning curse. Yet the scholar Murray Pittock has pointed out that there is eyewitness evidence which says that Charles Edward had to be led away from the field by Colonel O'Shea (on the orders of general Sullivan), screaming dramatically, 'They won't take me alive!' Even then he attempted to turn back to the battle and had his bridle led away by a Scottish officer named Major Kennedy. It was absolutely the right decision, even if it was imposed on the prince.

Whether it happened, Lord Elcho's personal attack on Prince Charles Edward Stuart represents an expression of the primal betrayal that was palpable among the Culloden survivors. David Wemyss was certainly embittered after the battle and believed that the cause was not irrevocably lost. His own journal relates him meeting the crestfallen Charles Edward four miles from the fatal battlefield in a disordered state of mind, blaming the defeat on treason and singling out some Scots under his command, paranoid that they would sell his head to London for £30,000. The prince, Elcho said, only cared for the Irish who were close to him. He told Elcho that he could go where he pleased; he himself was going to France. Elcho rebuked him at his lack of resolution, 'so little worthy of a prince of his birth'. Then he berated him for abandoning his whole people, having lost perhaps 1,000 men when he still had thousands of fighting men under him. These arguments made no impression and they parted, with the nobleman swearing never to have any more to do with him. In France, Elcho determined not to associate with the prince, but he was persuaded to meet him again by John Drummond, Duke of Perth. When he did make the effort, Charles Edward refused to see Elcho. There was perhaps good reason. Driven by desperation or weariness, Elcho had solicited agents of George II for a pardon when he arrived in Paris.

If the prince paranoically blamed the Scots, Wemyss himself had form in deep-seated hatred. In his youth he had been educated at Winchester College and during his time there it was noted that he professed dislike for all Irishmen, most Englishmen and a good many Scots. To be fair, his treatment in returning to his native land after a time on the continent would not have endeared him to the English populace. He was driven out of a theatre in London under a barrage of candles and apples and insulted as a 'French dog'. Like many of the key players in the murky Jacobite underground, the character of David Wemyss seems difficult to exactly determine. In response to his request for a pardon from the British government, several objectors raised stories that he had been particularly brutal while serving as a Jacobite officer. He was accused of cruelty to government prisoners of war and allegedly threatened to cut off the right arms of every enemy officer who had been captured. Such accusations were the common stock of government officials hoping to demonise Jacobite figures. One witness who saw him fighting at the Battle of Prestonpans states that he alarmed and disgusted people because he had an air of savage ferocity; but that hardly seemed misplaced on a battlefield.

While Lord Elcho has been largely forgotten, the legend of the fugitive Prince Charles Edward survived in uncomfortable romantic conjunction with the memory of the last battle fought on British soil. As an event, the Battle of Culloden stands bleakly alone. It left an indelible mark on the consciousness of the nation of Scotland and an enduring bitterness between Scotland and its neighbour England. Jacobitism would forever afterwards be integrated into the identity of Scotland and a component of its ongoing aspirations to control its own identity, whether as a devolved country or a fully independent nation. The battle also inspired a raft of Gaelic and English poetry and song, lamenting the death suffered there and sometimes the defeat of the Jacobite leader, Charles Edward Stuart. Yet in some sense, Culloden was the beginning rather than the ending of a Jacobite odyssey that has endured to the present, albeit the encounter was realistically the end of the struggle between the royal houses of Stuart and Hanover. Part of the reason Jacobitism survived in the popular imagination, apart from its strong appeal to romance and adventure, was the ambivalent allure it had for successive generations and the sense that Culloden was a shameful event that somehow did not settle the aspirations of those who rose up against the British state. As John Prebble pointed out, it is significant that no British regiment, who were so proud of their miliary victories, kept Culloden among their battle honours.

Chapter 3

The Loch Arkaig Treasure

Following the defeat of Culloden in April 1746, belated efforts were made by the French and Spanish governments to bolster the waning insurrection in Scotland. As many Jacobites realised with immense frustration, the French in particular had been highly ambivalent both before and during the uprising. A significant deployment of troops from France could have tipped the balance decisively in favour of the Stuarts and persuaded uncertain sympathisers to actively work for a restoration of the old dynasty, especially if they had landed in England. But divided counsels prevailed in the French government. It was one thing for some ministers of Louis XV to pay lip service to the Jacobites, gleeful that it discomfited the British government, but quite another to actively support invasion and risk reprisals from London. In the end, funds were promised because of continued pressure from Jacobite agents in France seeking to make the nation fulfil its long-standing promises of support. But the aid that was dispatched was both begrudged and hopelessly tardy.

No troops were sent, but some munitions and hard currency were sent to the Stuart supporters in Scotland. In March 1746 a French vessel named the *Prince Charles* was chased into a sea loch in Sutherland in the far north of Scotland by the British HMS *Sheeness*. The French ship was in fact a former British vessel, the *Hazard*, which had been captured by Jacobites in Montrose harbour some months before. On board the ship, according to some sources, was a huge hoard intended for the rebel cause. The crew of around 160 were French, Spanish, Irish and Scots. The ship's captain, Talbot, had hoped to land the money in friendly territory at Portsoy in Aberdeenshire, but he was spotted and pursued northward around the Scottish coast by four Royal Navy ships. The inlet known as the Kyle of Tongue was too shallow for the pursuing *Sheerness*, so Talbot steered his ship in there. But they were trapped in the sea loch, so Talbot ordered the treasure to be unloaded after being bombarded for several hours by the formidable twenty-four-gun *Sheerness*. The government ship got in touch with the loyalist Lord Reay, chief of the Clan McKay, and his men pursued the enemy who had disembarked with five barrels of gold. After a short skirmish, during which several men were lost on both sides, the Jacobite crew were captured. The ship was given back its old name of the *Hazard* and a fair portion of the Jacobite treasure was shared out by the local government military men, according to their rank. Tradition locally says that the French broke open the chests and scattered the loot in the heather and in Loch Hacoin. There was a scramble for the gold by soldiers and local civilians, but how much anyone stole away with unofficially is unknown.

The second attempt to help happened in the following month. This time around 40,000 gold coins, *louis d'ors*, were stowed on board two French privateers, *Le Mars* and *La Bellone*. The value was equivalent to around £5 million today. Two weeks after Culloden, the French vessels were attacked by the British warships *Greyhound*, *Baltimore* and *Terror* in Loch nan Uamh. During the exchange of fire, the foreign ships reached shore and their cargo was perilously unloaded. The fortune had been transported under the care of an Irishman named Brown, who was under instructions only to release the valuable cargo under the sign-manual of Prince Charles Edward. The prince was still in hiding and unaware of the precious cargo. It was yet another misfortune for his cause that he was not able to gain the money and use it to procure more support.

Brown incautiously landed, under pressure from the enemy vessels, and two senior Jacobites on shore, Lord John Drummond and Lord Elcho, determined that the money was desperately needed and should remain with them. Brown objected but was threatened with arrest. The British sailors watched most of the cargo disembark and then saw it transported into nearby woods. But the Highlanders undertaking this task could not resist broaching the barrels of brandy brought ashore and were soon paralytically drunk. Following the hasty unloading of the precious cargo, the French ships were attacked by the Royal Navy force and a large number of men were killed, though the British ships were fought off. The French vessels were hastily repaired and carried some leading Jacobites, including Lord Elcho, back to France.

Some reports say that there were seven casks of treasure brought ashore, though this number is disputed. The confusion could be because one cask was temporarily misplaced in the rush to get it all landed. This was later found by a boy, though £600 or £700 had been removed. In a rough accounting of the treasure written several years later, Dr Archibald Cameron recorded that 800 gold pieces were immediately stolen by 'a fellow who went abroad in one of those ships whose name was conceal'd by the Priest who had it from him in confession'. One entire cask was rumoured to have been spirited away by Coll MacDonell of Barrisdale, while the remaining ones were taken to a hiding place at Loch Arkaig. Two of the leading figures involved with managing the fund were John Murray of Broughton (who later gave himself over to the Hanoverian regime) and Cameron of Lochiel. Though both had the chance to escape in the French vessels, both declined. Broughton, it was said, stayed behind for the sake of the prince; Cameron remained for the sake of his clan.

Some of the clan leaders wanted the fortune to be divided up at once. But Murray promised to settle all arrears and provide payment for every wounded Jacobite soldier and for widows. There was no chance, after Culloden, that the money could be used to fund further military operations, although some hoped that the money would be used to provision a new gathering of loyal clans. Some of the treasure was sent to Lochiel with Dr Cameron. Under Murray's instructions, three kegs (containing 15,000 coins) were buried in the woods locally in different spots. Seeking to confound would-be robbers, six casks were carried about by the clans. Only half of them contained gold; the other three were loaded with stones to replace the three already buried in Cameron ground.

Murray of Broughton's caution regarding the French money contributed to uncertainty regarding its fate. He retained a large portion of it at this stage for what he deemed necessary expenses and then made some efforts to communicate with the prince who was on the island of Uist. He fell ill though and word did not reach Charles Edward. Various clan chiefs were let into the secret of the location until finally it fell to Cluny Macpherson to be the guardian of a significant part of the money. The tale that Cluny physically guarded the fortune in his ramshackle mountain hideaway known as Cluny's Cage can be dismissed on logistical grounds: the task of lugging all the coins across mountain territory and then secreting them in a cramped cabin would have been impossible, though it appears he did get some.

Most writers credit Cluny with being scrupulously honest, which would make him an ideal candidate for being custodian of the treasure. But this did not prevent Prince Charles Edward Stuart from being doubtful about him later. He summoned Cluny to France in 1755 and interrogated him closely about the fate of the hoard. Cluny, it seems, had been under the impression that he had a somewhat free hand in distributing the wealth to support the disadvantaged Jacobite faithful in the Highlands. Cluny Macpherson may have taken as much as 12,000 *louis*. Some he certainly distributed among clan chiefs to alleviate want in their areas. Small amounts were given out by him personally, such as 100 *louis* to the widow of a Keppoch chief who had died for the cause. Amounts were also given out at the specific request of the now exiled prince. Thievery was undoubtedly endemic in the poverty-stricken north of Scotland and many hands tried and some succeeded in getting a portion of the bonanza, including the notorious double agent Alastair Ruadh MacDonell, whose codename was Pickle.

Despite this, Charles Edward had doubts about Cluny and his treasure management and he was also suspicious about the fate of his silver plate, which had been abandoned after Culloden. Cluny had dutifully gathered some of this, though not before some had been looted, but Charles demanded the whereabouts of a casket of jewels, which Cluny denied ever having seen. The prince was still harping on about this after Cluny's death to his brother-in-law Donald Macpherson of Breachachie, who exported what gold remained to the Young Pretender in 1765.

By whatever means, the foreign gold began to be distributed throughout the Highlands. Clansmen who had some money from Cluny complained he was being too tight-fisted with his handouts, and some men bickered on account of receiving less than others. Clan vied against clan for a portion of the loot, and brother competed against brother. Various parts of the hoard were secreted elsewhere. Murray of Broughton, finding his part of the horde too cumbersome to transport, had some of it buried in the garden of a Mrs Menzies at Culdare. Murray was accused of being bewitched by the hoard by another leading Jacobite involved, Lord Elcho. Elcho states that the fortune persuaded Murray to remain in Scotland rather than flee abroad, which led to his ultimate downfall and ruin.

Yet another prominent leading Jacobite involved in the treasure from the beginning was Dr Archibald Cameron. He persuaded the reluctant French captains to let the gold go ashore and helped arrange its burial and protect some of it from young Clanranald. Like Cluny, Cameron was regarded with some suspicion by Jacobites in Europe regarding the fate of the treasure. Dr Cameron was among others at Rome in 1750 who gave a detailed account to the Young Pretender about his part in the lost treasure. Chief among those muddying the waters about the fate of the gold and casting aspersions on Cameron was British agent Alastair Ruadh MacDonell of Glengarry. The confusion of the times and rivalries of those involved hopelessly confused any investigation into the fate of the gold. There are discrepancies in the accounts of the treasure given by Cameron in 1750 and by Cluny five years later. A chief sum of contention was £6,000 held by Cluny at one stage, some of which was used by Dr Cameron for expenses while travelling in Europe.

Knowing about the gold from Murray, and probably other informants, it is a wonder that government troops did not discover and confiscate any sizeable part of the hoard. Cluny (who may indeed have kept some money for himself) stated in 1755 that Murray embezzled £3,000 of the fund. Soldiers did search the woods at Loch Arkaig and saw the footprints of the men who had concealed the gold.

Even though the burying was done very inexpertly, they did not find any of the treasure. Dr Cameron, according to one account, reburied it more securely and it remained in two places until it was given over to Cluny Macpherson. The amount given to this chief was reckoned as £12,000.

The French treasure smuggled into Scotland was an ingredient in the eventual downfall of Dr Cameron. He secretly visited Scotland in September 1749 with the purpose of consulting with Cluny Macpherson about the disposal of the hidden gold. Cameron was afterwards accused of plundering the loot for his own gain, which was almost certainly untrue. However, it seems that he did take a sum to assist his Lochiel kindred and around £300 for his own expenses. At least, this was the accusation made against Cameron by the turncoat Alastair MacDonell of Glengarry. Another tradition states that MacDonell himself looted the Arkaig treasure. He certainly set the leading surviving Jacobites in the Highlands against each other using the French gold as his weapon. The fact that the treasure's sometime guardian Cluny Macpherson was himself accused of taking some of the treasure by Dr Cameron adds another level of mystery to the already murky legend of this gold. Macpherson's role in this will be considered later.

But was the treasure really lost? Martyn Downer has recently claimed that the hoard was spirited away south to England by the Northumbrian Charles Selby of Earle, who acted under instruction from Prince Charles Edward in 1748 or 1749. The exiled prince was desperate for the money and instructed Cluny to hand it over to his agents, including the Irish Major Kennedy whom he sent to Britain to liaise on his behalf. By this time, 1748, through handing out sums to sympathisers and probably through theft, the great fortune had dwindled to £6,000. It was brought to the English border and then Selby himself made two perilous trips to deliver it to Jacobite agents in London. Even then, it was said that Major Kennedy have diverted part of this reduced sum (£800) to fund his entertainment at Newmarket races en route back to the continent.

Various modern adventurers have sought the scattered remains of the Jacobite gold in the Highlands and found precious little. There is a story that a few coins were found near Loch Arkaig in the 1850s, but not enough to make anyone rich. The only thing of value to have cropped up in recent years was the rediscovered testament of one Neil Iain Ruari, which was found in a bookshop in Winchester and then passed to the West Highland Museum. Neil wrote that he saw some men burying something secretly in Arisaig, Morar. He waited until they had gone, then searched the place, luckily finding a bag of gold coins, which he happily spirited away. The exact spot is unknown, but a forlorn remnant of the Jacobite treasure may safely lie there still.

The story of the lost treasure has faded into the mist of Highland folklore and there are various tales about its fate. One such story says that, in the area known as the Feadan Mór, north of Gairloch, there was a buried keg of gold that became visible only once every seven years. It was originally shipped over from France to help the Jacobite cause. To protect this treasure, it was entrusted to Duncan MacRae of Isle Ewe who had the gift of *sian* and could make objects or people invisible. With two friends he buried the keg, in readiness for the day when the prince would come and have need of it, though he never came to the district. Almost a century passed, when a woman herding cattle happened to be spinning worsted when she spotted the top of the keg sticking out of the ground. Excitedly, she stuck her distaff in the earth to mark the spot and hurried home to her township to tell the news, but when she returned with her neighbours there was no sign of the treasure.

If the legend of the lost gold, in one respect, retains a rosy, charming glow all these years later, there is of course another side to it. We are entitled to wonder what would have happened if that crucial cargo had reached Scotland earlier and reached the hands of those who could have used it to turn around the flagging impetus of the rebellion in the north of Scotland. In one sense, the story of the legendary kegs of gold is a rosy diversion from the sober main narrative of the Jacobites. Yet the story surely also represents another piece of ill fate in the bad-luck saga of the Jacobites. Those who search for it still in the Highland wastes are probably on a fool's errand. Who would want such a sad, tainted fortune, cursed with ill luck anyway?

Chapter 4

Executions and Atrocities

The shadow of the failure of the '45 rebellion naturally fell most across the scene of the conflict in Scotland. Tales of the barbarity of the government forces, led by the Hanoverian prince and commander the Duke of Cumberland, quickly spread and are still a matter of controversy. The nature of the retribution and barbarism inflicted by agents of the victorious British state against the defeated Jacobites may have been exaggerated, but there is enough surviving evidence to demonstrate cruelties imposed not only against defeated military opponents but also uninvolved civilians in the Highlands. In September 1746 there were 15,000 soldiers in Scotland and still 10,000 stationed there a year later, demonstrating the level of seriousness that Great Britain still viewed the Jacobite threat.

A major contributory factor in the merciless subjugation of the Highlands after Culloden was the fact that the majority of English people, as well as many Lowland Scots, perceived the inhabitants of the region as degenerate savages. Not only were they alien in language and culture, they were also treacherous. One Lowland correspondent in *The Scots Magazine* in July 1746 expressed ardent hope that the region should soon be righteously punished, even though the majority of the Highland population did not in fact actively support the Jacobites: 'Those miserable wretches who have been the rod of God's anger to chastise us for our sins: I mean the banditti that harbour in most of the Highlands of Scotland, that nursery of rapine and violence, where rebellion is always hatching, and brooding her cursed offspring.'

Dubious, racist distinctions were drawn between the civilised 'Saxon' areas of Scotland and the Highlands and Islands. The sharp distinction led to prejudices that were the basis of beliefs that the population should be punished, removed, or killed as needs be to make matters more peaceable for the greater good. The impetus to socially engineer the region was channelled through reason and economics. William Crosse, professor of law at Glasgow University, suggested in an essay in 1748 that the Highland region had three times as many people as were needed there for the simple task of rearing cattle (deemed to be the only worthwhile activity in the area), and the idle two-thirds of the populace therefore had nothing to do but thieve and indulge in other criminality. The condescending assertion that it was hardly their fault that they were hopelessly degenerate did not spare them the consequences of forced social change in the following decades, even if some of the change was viewed by outsiders as beneficial. Military reprisals were followed by language suppression, land 'improvement', resettlement and emigration.

The Act of Proscription in 1746 was a necessary piece of legislation, from the government's viewpoint, in pacifying a still potentially rebellious region of the country. People were forbidden to possess firearms, which prevented possible further armed insurrection but also deprived some of the ability to hunt game and pushed some households to the brink of starvation. Highland dress was banned (except for certain British serving soldiers), with a penalty of six months' imprisonment for offenders, with repeat offenders facing transportation abroad. A following act severed the power of clan chiefs by depriving them of their heritable powers in their own areas.

Military violence was undoubtedly a tool in cowing the region into submission. To what extent it was a policy imposed on the army by its leaders is still contentious. Modern efforts by some to rehabilitate the inherent brutality of William Augustus, Duke of Cumberland, son of King George II are disingenuous. Butcher Cumberland, as he was known, was allegedly responsible for particular mercilessness to Jacobite prisoners and non-combatants alike that went beyond the standard norms of eighteenth-century behaviour. An experienced young officer, he was understandably zealous in his hatred of the enemy, begging his father for command of the campaign against the insurgents. How far he strayed beyond accepted contemporary military protocol in the aftermath of Culloden is arguable. While the king wanted all Jacobite prisoners who were being taken to Carlisle to be transported to the West Indies and

America, his son contradicted his order and had many of them hanged. One government-supporting Presbyterian minister, who had heard about the widespread military murders in Scotland, wondered whether Cumberland was himself truly a Jacobite. His brutal campaign had caused so much outrage in Scotland that many people sympathised with the defeated Jacobites. Cumberland's reputation was almost immediately damaged. One of the first uses of the unflattering epithet 'Butcher' to describe him came not from quasi-treacherous Scots but from an alderman of London who objected to such a bloodthirsty figure being made a freeman of the city. Cumberland's celebratory statue in Cavendish Square, London, was removed by the Victorians; hearts and minds were by then fully behind the Jacobites.

Cumberland was a product of his time and the whole nation, in war and peace, was well used to violence throughout the eighteenth century. As Alvin Redman succinctly wrote: 'the English male was probably the most bloodthirsty man in Europe.' Robbery, riots, mob rule were all habitual in every town and city. Public hangings, the pillory, and other state-sponsored cruelties were popular public entertainment. The Jacobite uprising was seen as a criminal enterprise by traitors, and so were not treated as honourable opponents. Despite opposition to the Act of Union in 1707, a great many Scots were reconciled with a sense of Britishness and were loyal to the Hanoverian crown. Many atrocities in the Gaelic-speaking areas of Scotland were inflicted by Lowland Scots as agents of the British state, who needed little encouragement to be severe with their hereditary enemies. However, excusing brutality on the basis that it was a universal eighteenth-century phenomenon is disingenuous. Some leaders of the British army were notably humane when dealing with defeated Jacobites after Culloden. One was John Campbell, 4th Earl of Loudoun, who ordered his men not to 'destroy or distress' the country unless there was no other means of imposing order. Some Jacobites specifically sought Loudoun's protection before surrender, including a group of 100 men from the Cameron clan. Pro-government Highlanders like Duncan Forbes of Culloden and the Duke of Argyll also advocated peaceful means of disarming and pacifying the region. Yet, to Cumberland, Forbes was 'arrant Highland mad' and 'that old woman who talked to me about humanity'.

Was the 'rebel' army any better in its treatment of opponents? As a means of winning hearts and minds, the Jacobites frequently released captured British troops (with conditions), while the Hanoverian regime possibly could not afford such tolerance, being under an existential threat from a still potent, recently deposed rival monarchy. Christopher Duffy points out that the British military machine was equally ruthless in dispossessing French settlers in North America in the same period, unlike the French forces who were notably milder with those of British extraction under their jurisdiction. The good duke ('Sweet William' to some of his associates) was hardly the only guilty party in his sanctioning violence against unmilitary targets, nor were the English authorities unique in participating in the savageries of their times.

Murdering defeated and injured soldiers on the battlefield and nearby after battles was a common military tactic in Britain and elsewhere. Survivors sometimes had to thank either providence or sheer good luck for pulling through when so many of their comrades perished. Alexander Fraser was an ensign in the Master of Lovat's regiment and was carried with other wounded men after the battle to Culloden House. They were afterwards loaded into carts and Fraser assumed they were being taken to Inverness to have their wounds dressed. But the men were unloaded after a while and ranged on their knees against a wall and then shot. He fell with the others, assuming he had been hit. Most men who survived this fusillade had their brains dashed out. A soldier struck him with the butt of his rifle, shattering his jaw and nose and dislodging one of his eyes from its socket. Left for dead, he was luckily spotted some while later by Lord Boyd crawling away from the heap of bodies. The peer's servant carried him away to a nearby cottage where he was concealed until he recovered. Individual horror stories from this period are rife, but Jacobite propaganda may be responsible for creating some tales of massacres (notably, perhaps, the story of Jacobite captives burnt alive in a barn, according to author Jonathan Oates).

Killing the wounded on the battlefield and butchering fleeing defeated troops afterwards is one thing; slaying innocent men, women and children far from scenes of conflict is another. Rapes, killing of non-combatant males, burning of houses and crops, slaughtering of cattle – all of this certainly occurred. Some of the details of these outrages remain extremely affecting. There was Murdoch McRaw or Moran, a non-Jacobite who was taken to Inverness and accused of being a spy. The soldiers put a rope around his neck on an apple tree but he could not believe that they would hang him for nothing. Thinking it was some macabre game, he said to the soldiers, 'You have gone far enough if this be jest.' But they hanged him and his naked body was disgracefully displayed there for several days. It was said that he had the peaceful appearance of one who had fallen asleep. The same grotesque disbelief was displayed by three men in Glenevis, who were actually laughing when the nooses were put around their necks. Instances of women being raped by British soldiers and mariners were not uncommon in the Highlands and the Hebrides.

Many accounts of outrages, as well as other experiences of Jacobites, commoners and peers, are recorded in the testimony compiled by the committed Jacobite Bishop Robert Forbes of Ross and Caithness. His *Lyon in Winter*, not fully published until the late Victorian era, contains an astonishing amount of material relating to the Battle of Culloden, the prince's subsequent escape, plus details of those involved in the uprising. Though some of the eyewitness testimony and reports of war crimes are undoubtedly partisan or exaggerated, there is still much important material relating to the suffering of Stuart loyalists after their defeat. The rumour mill about the monstrous behaviour of the redcoats was working full time in the Highlands, though some reports of their supposed ogre-ish deeds are more akin to folklore than fact. The wife of Dr Cameron heard the British soldiers were digging up corpses, children included, to steal their linen shrouds and leaving their bodies exposed on the ground. There was gossip that British soldiers in some areas deliberately poisoned bread and left it for women and children to eat. The Young Pretender, when hearing about atrocities while he was on the run in the region, scarcely believed that the authorities could be capable of such depravity. The would-be Englishman could not believe what his countrymen were capable of.

Part of the retrenchment of the British establishment after the '45 included conspicuously executing captured leaders of the rebellion in

London. The headline proceedings caught the public imagination, as much for the behaviour and character of the accused as their heinous treachery. Among those condemned was Arthur Elphinstone, 6th Lord Balmerino, a long-time Jacobite who joked through his trial and met his death unrepentant, stating, 'If I had a thousand lives, I would lay them down in the same cause.' His nobility struck a chord with the disenfranchised sector of English society. Two years after his death the highwayman Thomas Neale, who also suffered the ultimate judicial penalty, declared he was as similarly hard done by as the noble lord. The connection – in English establishment eyes – between Jacobitism and criminality had been made very early in fact. James Whitney, executed in 1693, had started off as a butcher's apprentice and was conspicuously labelled a Jacobite, having plotted to assassinate the new Dutch king. His notoriety earned him a place in many broadsides and ballads. Other shady individuals were linked with the displaced Stuarts, such as the Waltham Blacks (poachers in Hampshire) and the Sussex smugglers. The latter were sounded out at one stage by leading Jacobite Sir James Harrington to see whether they could assist the cause.

Less dyed in the wool in his loyalties than Balmerino was William Boyd, 3rd Earl of Kilmarnock, who joined the Jacobites only on the pretext that it offered a possible means of advancement out of his own debt-ridden situation. Boyd is a prime example of one of those desperate men who followed the Stuart cause because they believed society under the Hanoverians had ill-served them. Although his wife was ardently Jacobite, Boyd was apolitical and later confessed to the Duke of Argyll, 'for the two kings and their rights, I cared not a farthing which prevailed; but I was starving, and, by God, if Mahomet had set up his standard in the Highlands, I had been a good Mussulman for bread, and stuck close to the party, for I must eat.' Despite this, he served Charles Edward well, becoming a colonel and a privy counsellor. He was captured at Culloden and only managed to escape immediate death by pleading for his life. Taken to London, his appeal for clemency failed and he was executed. His co-condemned, the Earl of Cromarty, did manage to appeal against his death sentence. Another to die was Charles Radcliffe, brother of the Earl of Derwentwater, who suffered the same fate after the uprising of 1715.

More fortunate than Kilmarnock was John Murray of Broughton, a leading Jacobite in the '45 who was taken prisoner and then notoriously turned king's evidence and informed on his former associates. Many Jacobite activists were betrayed by Murray; he also gave the government information concerning the elusive Loch Arkaig gold. Ironically known as Mr Evidence Murray, his notoriety followed him to his grave, and he was widely despised by Scots who had no Jacobite leanings. Sir Walter Scott's father represented Broughton in legal matters, but, and after each time Murray visited him, he would throw the cup he drank from out the window because he could not bear to retain a vessel such a man had used. According to Lord Elcho, although Murray had indeed been a staunch Jacobite, he principally encouraged Prince Charles Edward to venture to Scotland because he wanted the chance of 'fishing in troubled waters'. After his release from prison, Murray spent most of his life in London, Strangely, he seems to have met Charles Edward Stuart when the exiled prince came incognito to the capital in 1763. There is a fable that he ended up in an asylum where curious individuals paid money to come and stare at him.

Among the elder statesmen of the Jacobite cause were William Murray, Marquis of Tullibardine and Simon Fraser, Lord Lovat. Although in his late fifties during the campaign, Tullibardine had aged tremendously during a long and painful exile in France and could barely walk, and his practical part in the '45 was severely limited. He surrendered to British forces and was imprisoned in the Tower of London, where it is probably fortunate that he died of natural causes in July 1746 before he could face a treason trial. An altogether more complex man was Simon, Lord Lovat, who conducted himself with wry dignity through the legal proceedings. He had some of the personal allure of Charles Edward Stuart, though his charisma was decidedly dark. After he was sentenced to death, a stranger seriously offered his own life in execution in place of the condemned peer.

In common with some others, Lovat met his death bravely and was extremely courteous to those he met in the days before his death, the last peer to be publicly executed in Great Britain. He disdained to ask the king for mercy and declared that he would have lived for another twenty years if not for the axeman awaiting him. He was nearly 80 at the time. Though he retained his marked sense of humour, his dignity before death contrasted with some of his actions during his long and disreputable life. His final days were strangely marked by incident and black comedy. Shortly before his beheading, the scaffolding collapsed, ironically killing several of the bloodthirsty spectators who had come to witness the beheading. Taking this as an entertaining act of God, Lovat remarked when informed, 'Good, the more mischief the better the sport.' As he entered the carriage on the way to his death, an old woman stepped out and shouted, 'You will have your head chopped off, you ugly old Scots dog.' Lovat immediately turned to her, raised his hat, and laconically replied, 'I verily believe I shall, you old English bitch.'

Lovat examined the fatal axe before its use to test its sharpness and remarked about the sizeable crowd that he was surprised there should be such a fuss made about the removal of an old grey head. He informed the executioner if he wounded his neck and he was able to rise, he would be angry with him. *Dulce et decorum est, pro patrie mori*, the old lord declared on the block: it is sweet and proper to die for your country. Many Jacobites, upon reflection, realised it had been their nation rather than the Stuarts they were truly fighting for.

Chapter 5

Hiding in the Hills

For all the efforts of the British government, which were considerable, there were still men at large who had participated in the Jacobite uprising and remained active to differing extents after their defeat at Culloden. Sporadic local celebrations (admittedly small in scale) marked the birthday of the 'king over the water', James VIII. Weapons were still grudgingly being handed in by Stuart supporters into 1748, whose numbers were still evident and not only in the Highlands. A British officer dolefully noted in December 1747 that attainted rebels were still disgracefully appearing in public in the shires of Aberdeen, Banff and Angus. In the north, armed bands had still been roving the hills in the months immediately after Culloden, including 500 under Clanranald.

Some of those who actively supported the Stuart cause were lucky enough to placidly return to the communities they came from without recrimination. Others had to endure exile, fleeing to places like Norway and France, where many of them suffered hardship or death. For those who remained underground in their own country, there was the ghostly life of the internal exile. Some Jacobite men were forced into hiding, known to be in Scotland and sheltered by sympathisers, eluding the attentions of the authorities who desperately sought to find them. The Duke of Cumberland sent out an order to 'pursue & hunt these Vermin among their lurking Holes'. In a list sent to their commissioners in May 1746, the supervisors of excise in various parts of Scotland detailed the names and locations of those men in their districts who had been part of the rebel army. Over 2,000 men are named and just over 400 described as 'lurking'. Some others were 'skulking' in the hills, mountains or braes, or had location 'unknown' written next to their names. Only a few were noted to have escaped abroad. The list is patchy and likely inaccurate. Some of those in hiding were soon captured or escaped to Europe. It was not just in the Highlands that fugitives eluded authorities. The list from Montrose details men from Angus and the Mearns, a mix of low and high lands, where there were seventy-seven lurkers in a list of 335 targeted men. The stories of a few of these refugees from justice passed into local legend and they became as significant as the better-known Jacobite heroes. Some of those named in the lists were not soldiers, but had merely shown public support for the rebellion, or maliciously spoken about the king, such as the glazier David Henderson from Clackmannan, who had drunk the health of the Pretender's son and then assaulted an exciseman who reproved him. Some men were accused of harassing local communities or inducing people to join the Jacobites; others were admitted to have been forced into the rebel army. Fragmentary glimpses of the fate of some are afforded in the records. James Sinclair pursued the Jacobites when they advanced into England, hoping to retrieve horses they had stolen, but he had not reappeared after six months and it was feared he had been compelled to join their ranks against his will. Ministers supporting the Stuarts are also named. There was substantial friction in some areas between non-juring Episcopalians (who did not accept Hanoverian rule) and the established Church of Scotland. Kirks were burnt, ministers turned out, and there was harassment on both sides of the religious divide.

Those condemned to wander as hidden, nameless figures either in their own country or accept the bitterness of exile abroad, became not only shadows of their former selves, but almost so insubstantial as to become living ghosts. To borrow the nickname of the outlawed Clan Gregor, these uncaptured Jacobite rebels after Culloden were 'children of the mist'. Some of their names may never be known, nor their fates. Those who sought to evade capture and justice stood more chance of success in areas where Jacobite sentiment was still strong. Orkney was still not controlled by the government in May 1746 and in the Islands, there were at least four fugitive lairds who had been out in the rebel forces and went underground.

Those who chose an alternative to surrender were motivated by the barbarity meted out to many rebels who handed themselves in. Some of the circumstances of those who evaded the redcoats in Scotland are extraordinary. One of those who took to the heather was poet and clan leader Duncan Robertson of Drumachin (known as Strowan Robertson). His kinsman Alexander, 13th chief of Clan Robertson, fought in the 1715 rebellion and was obliged to flee abroad. Aged 75, Duncan heartily supported the '45, though infirmity meant that he was unable to accompany the Jacobite army on their ill-fated march into England. He remained staunch in his support of the Stuarts and was declared a fugitive. He skulked in the hills, glens and houses of friends until he was able to escape to Holland. From 1746 to 1753, as he later documented, he hid in no less than 157 locations in Scotland and was betrayed by no one who sheltered him.

James Carnegie of Balnamoon in Angus was a laird remembered by later generations for his humour, eccentric character and drinking as well as his ardent Jacobitism. During the rebellion the Jacobites appointed him Lieutenant Deputy of Angus. He was also the reputed composer of the popular song 'Low Down in the Broom'. After the Jacobite defeat, he reputedly went into hiding in the guise as a shepherd for some time and was accompanied at times by his younger namesake George Carnegie who sometimes had to carry the exhausted Balnamoon through the wild hills on his back. The laird's most famous refuge was Bonnymoon's (or Balnamoon's) Cave in Glen Mark. One evening he ventured into a local farmhouse and was sitting by the fire when a party of soldiers came in and enquired about the Laird of Balnamoon. Luckily, Carnegie was dressed as a poor servant and he listened anxiously while the farmer, James Mill, said he had not seen him. Mill then gruffly ordered Balnamoon to go and clean the byre, which he thankfully did, scurrying away from the presence of the redcoats.

Local legend says that Balnamoon was betrayed by the local Presbyterian minister, Reveren Scott. This cleric also had his Episcopalian rival, Reverend David Rose, a Stuart supporter, arrested and imprisoned in a ship lying off Montrose. As Scott was riding to a meeting of the local presbytery in 1749, his horse stumbled and threw him off. He was killed in the fall and some people noted with satisfaction the hand of divine intervention. The place where he was killed was beside the kirk of Rowan, an Episcopalian kirk he had caused to be destroyed. Carnegie adopted his wife's territorial designation of Arbuthnott of Findourie and became James Carnegie-Arbuthnott in 1745. This caused confusion over his identity when he was arrested; he was released in 1748 and lived until 1791. Some stories say that both James Carnegie and his relative George found refuge for some time in Gothenburg.

Jacobite rebels who had both money and a wide circle of friends who had influence in the community stood a far better chance of evading capture for longer than those common soldiers who had to depend on mere cunning for survival. One of the most exemplary upper-class evaders was Alexander Forbes, 4th Lord Forbes of Pitsligo. He was an extremely accomplished individual, who authored several well-regarded philosophical works, and had taken part in the Jacobite uprising in 1715 at the age of 37. Exiled in France after that defeat, he returned to Scotland in 1720 and showed considerable courage to throw his lot in with the Jacobites in 1745, when he was 67. He raised a company of cavalry from his home district and initially hid in a house in Fraserburgh after Culloden. He often had to conceal himself in natural hiding places, in his case most famously Lord Pitsligo's Cave, though at other times he had to cower below the cramped arches of an old bridge as decrepit as himself. Like other Jacobite fugitives, Pitsligo's narrow escapes also entered local folklore. During one episode on the road, he drew attention to himself from a group of local soldiers by having a violent asthma attack. However, he managed to convince them that his disguise as a beggar was his real identity and was released with a few pennies to see him on his way. Despite periodic searches for him, he later managed to live fairly quietly with his son in the district using the name of Mr Brown and died in 1762, aged 84.

Some lurkers were disadvantaged by nature when it came to attempting to conceal themselves. One such was Andrew Hay of Rannes in Banffshire who had the misfortune to be the conspicuous height of 7 foot 2. Hay ruefully wished that 'his height had been more moderate'. Exempted from the Act of Indemnity of 1747 that effectively pardoned some Jacobites, Hay had to be sheltered in his home district by his mother and the tenants on his estate. Like Balnamoon, he narrowly escaped capture on one occasion in a farmhouse, when he concealed his large frame under the covers in two beds. The farmer's wife explained the shape beneath the blankets to the searching soldiers as being both her maids who were simultaneously poorly. In 1752, Andrew departed for Holland and France, and endured a miserable peripatetic existence, longing to return to his homeland. It was eleven years before he was able to return to his home. Poverty and stress during his years abroad had affected his health, though he lived for another sixteen years. Still, he may have counted himself luckier than the many men who never saw their homes or families again.

Not all those rebels who remained at liberty in Scotland had the luxury of being able to rely on others to conceal them over extended periods. Some Jacobites took a more aggressive method to ensure survival. John Dubh Cameron had been a sergeant in the French army but returned to Scotland to fight for the Jacobite cause. After defeat he led a band of freebooters who preyed on landlords in the central Highlands, stealing cattle and imposing blackmail upon them. His crimes were partially justified on the basis that he claimed to be targeting those lairds who had been Jacobite enemies, though his actions can also be seen as the continuation of an occupation of thievery that went back centuries in the region. Cameron had all the attributes of a legendary figure, foremost of which were his bravery and cunning. He was also a huge man, known as the Sergeant Mór, a reference either to his physical size or his large personality. His usual hiding place was in a barn at Dunan in Rannoch, but here one night in April 1753 he was seized by a party of soldiers. Some say that he was betrayed by the owner of the property who stole away his weapons. Cameron was surprised in his sleep but managed to fight off the troopers who entered the barn. However, he was outnumbered and badly beaten by the soldiers outside and he was carried off. He was tried for murder, theft and cattle raiding, and executed at Perth in November 1753. The court official who came to lay hands on Cameron shrunk in fear when he threatened violence.

Due to his activities and supposed Robin Hood tendencies (never preying on the innocent or poor), the sergeant's deeds inevitably passed into legend. There was a story of him encountering an officer from Fort William who was lost in the mountains of Laggan. He confessed to Cameron that he was carrying a large sum of money for the garrison and that he was fearful of meeting the Sergeant Mór. The officer and the incognito fugitive fell into talking about the exploits of the sergeant. Their conversation carried on until the Englishman referred to him as a thief and murderer. 'Stop there,' interrupted his companion, 'he does indeed take the cattle of the Whigs and Sassanachs, but neither he nor his *kearnachs* ever shed innocent blood; except once, that I was unfortunate at Braemar, when a man was killed, but I immediately ordered the *creach* [the spoil] to be abandoned, and left to the owners, retreating as fast as we could after such a misfortune.' The officer was alarmed and asked his identity. 'I am John Dubh Cameron,' came the reply. 'I am the Sergeant Mór; there is the road to Inverlochy; you cannot now mistake it. You and your money are safe. Tell your governor to send in future a more wary messenger for his gold. Tell him also, that, although an outlaw, and forced to live on the public, I am a soldier as well as himself, and would despise taking his gold from a defenceless man who confided in me.' The soldier gladly scurried off and told his story to his awe-stricken comrades when he found safety. Folk hero though he may be in Highland memory, one recent authority, Alan Macinnes, has bluntly described Cameron as a 'contract killer'. He was undoubtedly, in the eyes of the authorities, a troublesome leader of a band of caterans, or thieves. Cattle theft was always an easy default occupation for marginalised men in the Highlands.

Parallels can be made with Stuart loyalists in Ireland who opted to remain at home rather than flee to Europe. Whether such men would have ended up as criminals eventually under any regime is another matter, but being both Jacobite and an outlaw gave a double dose of dangerous mystique to some individuals. In Ireland, some bands of irregular troops known as *rapparees* supported the Stuart cause during the Williamite war. Following defeat, many members of the guerrilla bands drifted into criminality to sustain themselves. The term also became used for troublesome gangs, some of whom had Jacobite loyalties. In Cork, Donal na Cása O'Keefe was forced to flee to the fastnesses of the countryside and become a cattle thief, a profession that did not diminish his popularity in the neighbourhood. One of his hideouts was a cave concealed by the River Blackwater, which he used as a base to terrorise the rich of the district.

Such men's devotion to the latter Jacobite cause was sometimes notional or secondary to their banditry. Numerous outlaws gained fame and notoriety for being focal points for community resistance to incomers and English authority, such as Edmond O'Ryan or Eamonn a Chnoic (Ned of the Hills), active in both west Tipperary and east Limerick. Shane Crossagh O'Mullan, active in Northern Ireland in the first two decades of the eighteenth century, pursued a purely individual agenda. Others seem to have maintained some parallel affiliation to the cause, such as Seamus McMurphy, poet, criminal and Jacobite, who actively schemed to support the Stuarts in the mid-eighteenth century, but who ended up on the gallows in 1750. A latter-day figure following the same tradition was Black Francis McHugh (Proinsias Dubh), a bona fide folk hero who allegedly followed the template of enduring popularity by robbing the rich and giving to the poor in his native County Tyrone. Hero or heinous outlaw, he inevitably met the hangman all the same and bravely met his end around 1780. Troublesome through such gang leaders were, they did not come close to causing instability to society and their contribution to Jacobitism was minimal. The *rapparees* represent a social phenomenon that was a reaction to dispossession of native landed families which arose in the seventeenth century and continued into the eighteenth century. Whole gangs as well as individuals were troublesome to the law. These included the Munster Whiteboys and other, more family-based bands. Because popular sentiment in song and verse favoured the exiled royals as well as praised banditry, the two became fused in the Protestant enemy's imagination.

In Scotland, another Scottish Jacobite folk hero was John Roy (or *Ruadh* Stuart), described by a Victorian literary Scot as 'the beau-ideal of a clever Highland officer'. He also conformed to that wider Scottish ideal of being able to excel at many things: he was a 'lad o' parts'. Soldier, adventurer, exile, poet, he was also beloved by Bonnie Prince Charlie, who called him 'the Body'. When the fugitive prince was hiding in the cunning refuge known as Cluny's Cage, he heard that John Roy was approaching and wrapped himself under a plaid. When he jumped out to surprise John as he entered, the latter cried out, 'Oh, Lord! My master,' and fell in a faint.

Like several other conspicuous Jacobite stalwarts, Stuart initially pursued a military career in the regular British army, becoming a lieutenant and quartermaster in the Scots Greys. It was only after he was turned down for a commission in another regiment that he reconsidered his loyalties. He was imprisoned for Jacobite sympathies in 1736 but escaped from Inverness gaol with the connivance of the Sheriff of Inverness, Lord Lovat, who himself had notable anti-Hanoverian tendencies. Stuart even stayed at Lovat's residence for several weeks and the two entertained themselves by composing rip-roaring Jacobite verses. John Roy eventually relocated to France and joined the Royal Écossais and fought in the Battle of Fontenoy in Flanders in May 1745, coming home to support the uprising in Scotland in the same year. He raised the Edinburgh Regiment for the rebels and fought in all the engagements in Scotland. An English opponent who observed him at Culloden remarked, 'if all the Highlanders had fought as well as the officer with the red head and the little hand, the issue might have been different.'

After the Jacobite defeat, he went into hiding in the high country like so many others and also took refuge in a cave, named after him, on Craiggowrie, Strathspey. He was forced to take refuge in various places before he met with Prince Charles on Ben Alder and went over the seas to France with him, dying there in either 1747 or 1752 (the sources disagree). His considerable reputation as a Gaelic poet lingered long after him. Tales of such shadow men in the wilderness have endured in folktales, obscuring the real hardships and struggles by such outlaws.

The prize for the longest-lasting period of lurking without capture in Scotland post-Culloden by any prominent Jacobite must go to Cluny Macpherson, who was on the run in Scotland for the best part of a decade. While his adventures were romantic and colourful, they involved real suffering that went beyond his own privations. Known locally as Ewen Bán, and called Cluny from his residence, his family estate was seized by the government; his tenants loyally continued to pay their rents to him also, a crippling double burden not unique after Culloden. Cluny Castle was burned down by the government in June 1746 and his broken father died in the same month. His wife lived in a small house nearby, visiting him clandestinely. A price of 1,000 guineas was on his head with eighty government soldiers stationed in his home district to root him out, which they never did. His popularity went beyond clan loyalty (he was son of the chief of Clan Macpherson), and he emerged from the '45 with the reputation of having the greatest integrity of any of the leading Jacobites. Cluny came to the Jacobite camp by rather circuitous means, allowing himself to be captured by their army and attempting to decoy the British government into thinking he was an unwilling participant in the rebellion. Prior to this event he had been an active supporter of the government and actively assisted General John Cope. But he soon became one of the most ardent and successful military leaders in the campaign and was a colonel in the Jacobite forces just two weeks after he was captured by them.

Luckily for him, he was not present at the Battle of Culloden for he was commanding 600 men who were guarding the mountain passes in Badenoch. He led his contingent towards the battlefield, but they were too late to participate; their presence may have made some difference to the outcome that day. Following the defeat, he returned to his native territory, sheltered by the populace. As many as a hundred people are estimated to have known his hiding places but he was never betrayed though there was a £1,000 price on his head. A local tradition states that his exact location was known to four trusted people only, including his piper James Macpherson, and these provided all his provisions. If any of his friends, and even his wife, wanted to know where he was at any time, they had to go through these four.

The government commissioned the Highlander Sir Hector Munro to root out Cluny, but he was unsuccessful. Cluny frequented the houses of relatives and supporters by day and slept in several different hideaways during his long itinerant life as a fugitive. One of his hiding places was Cluny's Cave, high on the steep rocky face of Craig Dubh about three miles from Cluny Castle. The artificial cave, *Uamh Chluanaidh*, was excavated by clan members who deposited the spoil in Loch Ovie below, and it was large enough to accommodate two or three men. This lonely cave still exists. One day a servant lad was on his way to the cave carrying some venison stew for his master when he was apprehended by some English soldiers who had been out looking for Cluny and guessed that the meal was for him. They threatened the boy with death if he did not lead them to where the wanted man was hiding. So, the servant led them over the hills for several weary miles and at length he seems to have diverted their attention by admiringly questioning them about their arms and equipment. He was especially fascinated by the large drum carried by one of the troopers, which he pretended to believe was actually a large cage. His naivety was enhanced by wondrously questioning the drummer in broken English, after which the musician played a few beats on his drum. The boy appeared to be awestruck and said he would give the man his venison stew if he was allowed to play the drum himself. His wish was granted and he beat the drum so loudly that the hills and the whole countryside heard the military beat. Cluny of course heard the drum and took the opportunity to vacate his cave. When the searchers reached the site they found it empty and none of them suspected the innocent-looking servant lad of warning his master.

Another manmade refuge of Cluny's was an underground bunker by the River Spey. A tale states that Cluny was hiding here one day when a passing man caused the roof to collapse, and the stranger tumbled in beside him. The two men fought and Cluny reached for his dirk, then relented and made the man swear never to reveal his refuge. After the man did so, Cluny thought better of his mercy and scurried off to another hiding place at Dalchully. He was unsurprised when the redcoats soon swarmed around his underground lair. Tales of narrow escapes swarm around the legend of Cluny, as they do with the other Jacobite lurkers, and it seems churlish to cast doubt on any of these tales. Possibly the nearest that Cluny came to capture was when he was visiting the small cottage where his wife resided after Cluny Castle was burnt down. The house was suddenly surrounded by soldiers on Munro's orders. There was no chance of immediate escape, so Cluny changed clothes in the kitchen with one of his servants and went up to the commander of the troops who was approaching the door and held the stirrup while he dismounted from his horse. Did he know where Cluny was, the commander asked? No, Cluny answered, but if he did, he would not tell him. The officer examined him closely, then said, 'Indeed, I believe you would not,' then added condescendingly, 'You are a good fellow; here's a shilling for you.'

Cluny's most famous place of refuge was a manmade bothy or shelter built from interleaved branches and other materials on Ben Alder. It was invisible from anyone passing below due to being built in thickets of holly and disguised with moss to match the mountainside, and it was a two-storeyed structure large enough to shelter half a dozen men. This cunningly constructed hiding place, Cluny's Cage, was home to Bonnie Prince Charlie also for six days in early September 1746 just prior to his escape to France. Robert Louis Stevenson also had his protagonists David Balfour and Alan Breck Stewart visit the Cage in his novel *Kidnapped*. This hideaway has fascinated historians for many years because of its royal associations, ingenuity and the stories of Cluny's lonely internal exile here. There is also a dispute about its exact location, since its structure likely disintegrated long ago. Affleck Grey and others who had intimate knowledge of this part of the Cairngorms rejected the generally held identification of the site with the place marked on maps as Prince Charles's Cave. He and others favoured the place known as Peregrine's Rock on west Ben Alder. Cluny managed eventually to escape to France in 1755, though his health like others who had been living a fugitive lifestyle was broken. A meeting with the broken Bonnie Prince Charlie was clouded by his suspicion of the missing money. Cluny's wife managed to join him in 1757 and they were together until Cluny's death at Dunkirk in February 1764, aged 58.

While perhaps dozens of hunted Jacobites hid in their native land, with various degrees of success, the country in which they hid was undergoing an irreversible change. The kilt and weaponry were outlawed and military rule superseded local authority. More insidiously, Popish and Episcopalian systems of religion were rooted out and the teaching of Gaelic was discouraged. Over forty estates belonging to Jacobite landlords were seized and efforts were made by the British state to enforce the weight of accepted civilisation upon the barbarous *Gaeltacht*. Like Ireland, Highland Scotland paid the same heavy price as a penalty for maintaining its own cultural identity for so long in the face of the homogenous British identity.

Chapter 6
Exiles

The dislocation caused by the defeat of the final Jacobite uprising of 1745–46 sent shockwaves through areas that had been most loyal to the Stuarts. The result was felt bitterly in parts of Ireland and Scotland, which suffered wider consequences as a result of the loss. Common soldiers mostly faced arrest and either transportation or execution, though many either went on the run or had the good luck of returning home without any consequence. Large numbers of men escaped abroad and made do with whatever lives they found there.

The Irish had a bitter advantage over the Scots because several generations of countrymen loyal to the Stuarts had migrated to France and maintained a powerful exiled network there. Following the unsuccessful campaign of James II in 1690 in the Williamite wars, huge numbers of the Irish Jacobite army, the Wild Geese, were allowed to migrate to the continent after the Treaty of Limerick in 1691. Many of them entered French service and others went to Spain, where some of them formed the personal guard of Philip V. One of their leaders was Patrick Sarsfield, first Earl of Lucan, a charismatic figure who was remodelled by some later nationalists as an Irish hero. Rather like the Scottish Jacobite icon Claverhouse, Sarsfield was a divisive figure, and part of his enigma was due to a lack of information about his life, which allowed later writers to colour him various shades of good and bad according to their own prejudices. King James II was wary of his motives, but he successfully led some 19,000 Irish military men to Europe. Like many Jacobite heroes, he assured his own legend by dying heroically, succumbing to wounds at the Battle of Landen in 1693. There was some wonder among Europeans, seeing the bravery and capabilities of Irishmen in their armies, that they had not been able to withstand the Williamite forces in their native land. It came down to divisions in leadership and poor as much as ill fate.

There may well have been some resentment among the Irish that they did not get a proportionate share of the exiled court's subsidy by the time they arrived in France in significant numbers. Besides this, their influence was weak because the English and Scots had already divided up the highest positions in the household of the exiled court at St Germain. Between 1688 and 1692, it is estimated that there were 40,000 Jacobite exiles in France alone. Sixty per cent of this number were displaced Irish. The number of Scots only dramatically increased after the failure of the uprising of 1715. For well-connected Jacobites landing in the favoured nation of France following the rebellions of 1715 and 1745, there was a long-established network of support, so they could hope to rely on other Jacobite exiles.

Others were less fortunate and some who had been officers in the rebel armies found they had no option other than to seek further service as private soldiers in the French regiments. This was a recurring issue for those who had been compelled to leave Britain and Ireland for France because of their political affiliations. The exiled King James II expressed concern for the Irishmen who had initially found no place in military service in France. When he protested to King Louis, some officers were allowed to join the French army, albeit they had to serve as privates. Queen Mary Beatrice disposed of some of her jewels to support indigent newly arrived supporters. Poverty was naturally a greater risk for those exiles without influence or connections on the continent, but there were exceptions to the general rule that upper-class Jacobites seldom lapsed into poverty. One who did was William Murray, Marquis of Tullibardine, heir to the Earl of Atholl. He participated in the 1715 and 1719 uprisings and ended up in France. Although supported by his family, he lapsed into destitution and suffered from severe mental and physical illness. Despite this, he survived to take part in the 1745 uprising.

Those Jacobites who arrived in Europe in the wave of failure following the 1745 uprising found there fewer resources from the Old and Young Pretenders to meet their basic needs. Many upper-class refugees from Scotland sought commissions in the military, some in Irish units. There was a suggestion that clan leader Donald Cameron of Lochiel would form a regiment from his own exiled followers. One Scottish regiment that did form was under the auspices of Lord Ogilvy of Airlie, an Angus nobleman. John Drummond, son of the Duke of Perth, formed the Royal Scots regiment in France in 1743, and it served as a haven for Scots who had previously joined their countrymen in Dutch service; one reason was that many did not like to serve under Irish officers. Later, some Scots soldiers left the Netherlands and joined the French-based regiment. Ironically, when the Royal Scots disbanded in 1762, its men were integrated into Bulkeley's regiment of the Irish Brigade.

Even those from the nobility and monied classes were not guaranteed success in a foreign land. One issue was that there were two shadow Jacobite courts. In Rome, King James III and VIII presided over a faded retinue of retainers who had mostly long ago lost hope of returning to power in Great Britain. His son, Charles Edward, hardly provided a stable focus that would have allowed loyal followers to orbit around. Not only was he geographically and financially insecure, being eventually kicked out of France, his increasingly dissolute lifestyle did not encourage loyal Jacobites to retain close bonds with him. The hero of the '45 was also suspicious of the motives of many of his followers, especially where matters of money were concerned. The unseemly double dealing that attended investigations into the fate of the vanished Loch Arkaig gold was symptomatic of the distrust among some senior exiled Jacobites. Infighting was endemic among senior dispossessed Stuart supporters in France and elsewhere.

The psychological strain of exile undoubtedly brought out the worst in some personalities that were already dubious. We can cite the case of William Macgregor of Bohaldie, for instance, who came from exemplary Jacobite stock, on the face of it. His father was Sir Alexander Macgregor and his mother was a daughter of Sir Ewen Cameron of Lochiel. He escaped to France soon after the Battle of Sheriffmuir in 1715 and became an agent of James Francis Stuart in 1740. Murray of Broughton described him memorably as 'the descendant of a cobbler, himself a broken butter and cheese merchant, a stickt doctor, a Jack of all trades, a bankrupt indebted to all the world, the awkwardest Porter-like fellow alive, allways in a passion, a mere bully, the most forbidding air imaginable'. He was accused of raiding the baggage train at Sheriffmuir and was succinctly summarised by Lord Elcho as 'a low lifed fellow devoid of truth'. Charles Edward warned his father against him in 1745, but James considered him 'an honest and sensible man'.

There was a flourishing community of Irish and Scots on France's Atlantic coastline, engaging in a range of mercantile activities, from cargo shipping to privateering and the slave trade. The traders kept links with their countrymen, especially those linked with their common cause, but the political affiliations quickly melted away after Culloden. Some earlier exiles, or at least those with resources to build upon, seem to have been energised by the unexpected opportunity to begin new lives. Among the Irish ex-patriots, Sir Charles Wogan stands out as the most buccaneering. Leaving Ireland in 1712, he took part in the 1715 rebellion and was imprisoned in London but escaped along with other rebel prisoners. He escaped to Europe and became attached to the exiled Stuart court. His most daring exploit was arranging the escape of the Old Pretender's future wife Clementina in 1718. She had been forbidden from marrying the Stuart prince by the Holy Roman Emperor under pressure from the British. But Wogan and a small band of associates smuggled her over 150 miles to Italy in a hugely impressive feat of cunning. Wogan later migrated to Spain and enjoyed a highly active and successful military career and later became governor of Barcelona. He had been keen to participate in the 1745 rebellion, but illness prevented him from journeying to Scotland with Prince Charles Edward and he was hampered in sending Irish reinforcements to aid the uprising. By the time he had recovered sufficiently and journeyed to Paris to venture to Britain to aid the cause, the rebellion was on the back foot, and Culloden of course killed his plans. He returned to Spain and died there sometime after 1752. Other prominent Irishmen serving in Spain included James Butler, 2nd Duke of Ormonde, who became a general in the Spanish army.

Several high-ranking Jacobites found similar important positions in various parts of the world. One of these was George Keith, 10th Earl Marischal. Following the failure of the 1715 uprising he left his native north-east Scotland and followed the Stuart monarchy to France. He commanded Spanish forces in the next Jacobite expedition in 1719 and was badly wounded, but managed to escape back to Spain. He enjoyed a long and varied diplomatic career afterwards, notably serving the Prussian monarch Frederick the Great. Although he kept his hand in Jacobite intrigue for many years, he did not play any part in the '45. He had a poor opinion of the young prince. When he returned to Scotland in 1761, his reception was less than cordial. Ironically, he was not ill-regarded primarily by those supporting the Hanoverian monarchy, but by some who had Jacobite sympathies and who regarded his non-participation in the last rebellion as tantamount to treason. Keith's younger brother James ventured even farther afield in his exile, serving in the Russian imperial army and becoming governor of Ukraine, though he later became active in Prussia.

Unlike Keith, most exiled Jacobites did not have the opportunity to revisit or resettle in their homelands. Those few who did were liable to find a jarring disconnection between themselves and their altered country. Family loyalties were sometimes divided, either based on economic sense or out of personal convictions, but those families that committed multiple members to the cause suffered severely. The Leith family from Leith Hall in Aberdeenshire was a conspicuous Jacobite kindred, with four brothers fighting for Prince Charles in 1745. Captain Lawrence Leith was one of two brothers jailed and allegedly transported to the West Indies (though some accounts dispute this), who managed to find their way home eventually. When he was whimsically asked what would happen to rebels in the afterlife, he replied that he had once dreamed that an angel questioned him what church he had attended on earth. He truthfully answered that he had attended none. The angel frowned and asked him his name and address. 'I hae nae name,' he said. 'I'm only a puir, auld nameless, hameless rebel.' Then the angel smiled and admitted him to heaven.

One usually congenial destination for those fleeing defeat in Scotland was Scandinavia. There were several reasons for seeking refuge in these northern nations. Geographically, they were relatively easy to reach for individuals fleeing by sea from the Northern Isles, Hebrides and the northern and eastern parts of mainland Scotland. The Protestant culture there was also sympathetic to Episcopalians, who otherwise would have had to find refuge in Catholic nations farther south. Also, there had been Jacobite activity in Scandinavia long before the 1745 rebellion. The

Swedish monarch Charles XII became a supporter of James Francis, the Old Pretender. In this he was supported by a range of influential Swedes including the statesman and visionary mystic Emmanuel Swedenborg. When King Charles died in Norway in 1718, he was planning a Jacobite-Swedish invasion of Scotland. Swedenborg and others believed that he had been killed by a Hanoverian assassin. This underhand murder theory was allied with other strange rumours. One account states that the dead king came to his surgeon in a dream and said that he had been slain by 'one who came creeping'.

Whatever the truth of that, the Jacobite links to Sweden were longstanding. The nation was one hotbed in which a particular Tory and pro-Stuart variant of freemasonry flourished, allowing a business and clandestine network to connect like-minded individuals in the north. Links between Sweden and Scotland were strong from the mid-seventeenth century and continued well into the eighteenth century. There were plans to send a military contingent to aid the 1745 effort and as late as 1752, there were rumours that another Jacobite invasion of Great Britain was imminent, and its troops would include a large number of Swedish regular soldiers.

Many Scots had established businesses in Scandinavia, especially at Gothenburg and Malmö, and in Copenhagen and Bergen. Gothenburg had been the home of a community of Scottish traders since the early seventeenth century. Jacobite political refugees were welcomed by communities that shared sympathies with them. In 1746 and 1747, forty-four displaced Jacobites arrived in Gothenberg and were welcomed. The British authorities were anxiously concerned as late as 1755 of rumours of active Swedish state support in another Jacobite invasion, though it came to nothing. Malicious reports also insisted that the Young Pretender himself was in Sweden three years later plotting trouble against Great Britain.

Among notables to end up in Sweden was John Mackenzie, Lord Macleod, who had the misfortune (or perhaps good luck) to be taken prisoner by the British a day before Culloden. He was pardoned of treason on condition that he surrender all rights to the earldom of Cromartie, of which he was the heir. He went abroad and connected with the exiled

Earl Marischal, who arranged a commission in the Swedish army. He served for a long period as a high-ranking officer there and also entered the Prussian military. After his return to Scotland, he became colonel of a British regiment and served in the Far East. Unlike many Jacobites, he was able to repurchase his family estates and restore the reputation of his line.

Another Scandinavian refugee was James Moir, Laird of Stoneywood in Aberdeenshire. Following the '45 he spent some time in Scotland under an alias and took up a trade repairing shoes. He narrowly escaped when his home was raided by soldiers, who were not overly keen to uncover him. The leader of the search party helpfully advised his wife, 'In case of another visit from us you had better remove the portrait of the *cobbler* from the dining room.' In November 1746 he embarked with other wanted men on a sloop for Norway and then migrated to Sweden, living at Stockholm as a naturalised citizen. He returned to Britain after sixteen years but seems to have taken a risk as he was never officially pardoned. Moir died peacefully in 1782. In Scotland he supported the widow of the cobbler who had sheltered him; she and her five children lived in his house at Stoneywood.

The most astonishing Swedish-Jacobite connection centres around a group of British pirates who were living an embattled existence on a small island off the island of Madagascar in the Indian Ocean. Hounded by Great Britain and other maritime powers, the pirates had been trying to buy their way out of their besieged home by offering their services to several nations, none of which wanted such desperate allies. Sweden had begun negotiations with the pirates in 1717. The pirates promised the Swedes large sums of money if they would let their associates attack British vessels in Swedish waters. Although some pirates did enter talks with Sweden, the prime mover in the scheme was a hustler named William Morgan, who had no substantial links with the pirate colony. Morgan had been an active Jacobite who fled to Brittany in 1715 and networked extensively with Irish Jacobites there and had commercial links with Sweden. By 1718, it was proposed that a Swedish East India company be based at St Marie, Madagascar, and compete with the lucrative companies sponsored by the British and Dutch. Following the death of

King Charles XII, Swedish interest in the Madagascar scheme waned and Morgan sought Spanish backing for different schemes in the West Indies and the Pacific. When this too failed, the enterprising Morgan approached the Old Pretender in 1720 and speculatively sought support, though the scheme was not defined. Morgan hoped to send ships and men to support the Jacobite Atterbury Plot in England in 1721, but this too fell through; he antagonised his Swedish supporters whose enthusiasm for the Jacobites had now dissipated. Some unhappy Swedish officials spread the rumour that the Madagascar trading scheme involving the pirates had in fact been a Jacobite plot to defraud their nation. Uncovering details of the pirate scheme is frustrated by the duplicity of those involved and the clandestine nature of their interaction. The supposed envoy of the Madagascar enclave was captain Simon St Leger, who did not actually have authority to speak for them. When he was told to go and get a commission from the pirates, he vanished, though his son Samuel found employment with a Swedish privateer in 1716. The latter may have been the privateer of that name who was working for the Swedish authorities and actively trying to ship arms to Ireland and Scotland to support the Jacobite cause.

Another privateer who did actively serve Sweden was the Liverpool-born John Norcross, a rival of Morgan's, who tried to get backing for his own version of the Indian Ocean trading scheme. Also an active Jacobite, he brought proposals of partnership from two genuine Madagascar pirates he encountered in France. Unlike Morgan, Norcross was a long-standing seafarer, but like many pirates his personality and character wrecked any credibility he had with others. Described by one person as a 'mad fellow' and by another as 'scatter-brained', Northcross escaped a death sentence in 1719 but ended up being captured in Denmark and committed to life imprisonment, dying in 1758. Scatter-brained or not, there is evidence that Norcross also plotted on behalf of Russia in a pirate-Jacobite plan that also came to nothing. The death of Charles XII put an end to the Indian Ocean dream. One incidental result of all this scheming was the establishment of the Swedish East India Trading Company, whose members included several mainly Scottish Jacobites.

There were some parallels between piracy and the Jacobites also in the western hemisphere. Some of those pirates who plagued shipping around Bermuda in the early eighteenth century were largely brought under control by British authority, but those who refused to cease their activities were confined to the island of New Providence. A large proportion of these renegades avowed allegiance to the Jacobite cause, though this allegiance to the exiled 'king over the water' was mostly an extension of the rebellious lifestyle that involved defying authority. Those with the strongest pro-Stuart views did manage to communicate with the Irish Jacobite admiral George Camocke in Europe and hatch a scheme to capture the archipelago in the name of King James III, but a new governor in the islands arrived and subdued piratical activity. The exiled king immediately expressed doubt anyway about the validity of the scheme and correspondence described one piratical figure involved as 'a little wrong in the head', which seems a common trait for members of his profession. Several pirates, such as the Scot Alexander Dalziel (hanged in 1715), ranged widely over the globe and offered fleeting allegiance to the exiled Stuarts, though their affiliation was based on expediency and was one part of a portfolio of loyalties they declared during their careers.

While Sweden was friendly to Jacobites, Norway (under the Danish crown) was not always so. A group of thirteen Scottish officers landed there on 24 May 1746 and were imprisoned on the recommendation of the British consul. Despite claiming to be merchants bound for Sweden, it was clear that they were Jacobite military refugees. Their leader was David, Lord Ogilvy, and the others were mostly Angus lairds, who had fled to sea in their dilapidated little barque at Dundee. After a while they were able to wander freely around Bergen, then contrived to escape to Sweden in a ship with a secret compartment, aided by the French consul. Ogilvy later went to France and took issue with the French in Bergen who had extorted money from the group. The captain of the Scots ship, James Wemyss, returned to Dundee and pleaded that he had made the North Sea journey under duress.

Another arrival who had an even more fraught experience was John Gordon of Glenbucket. With a price of £1,000 on his head, the Jacobite general escaped Scotland disguised as a beggar, and crossed difficult

Norwegian terrain on foot and by sled, an ordeal for a 74-year-old. He nearly perished in a town just over the Swedish border, but recovered and journeyed on to France where he died several years later. Old Glenbucket, as he was known, was not only active in the '45, but had participated in the 1715 campaign. He must surely have been the only man to have fought at both the Battle of Killiecrankie in 1689 and in the '45. Another of his ventures was an unsuccessful attempt to persuade the Old Pretender and the French to launch a Jacobite campaign in 1728. The rumour that George II had nightmares about him is probably untrue.

Russia was another popular destination for Jacobites who were, in some cases, recruited along with others by this nation to attract experts from the west in various fields, which would bolster the effort to modernise rapidly. Until his death in 1725, Tsar Peter the Great competed with other regional powers like Sweden and some of the German states for mastery. He considered practical support to help the exiled Stuarts regain power in Great Britain, but whether he would have ever followed this through is difficult to say. At one stage he proposed marrying off his daughter to the Old Pretender. Matters for the Jacobites in the region were hampered by the fluctuating state of Russian-Swedish relations. Various vagabond Jacobites, Scots and Irish, military and medical men, ended up in Russia as flotsam, having drifted through various places in Europe. The Russian navy recruited many men from the British Isles, not all Jacobites, throughout the eighteenth and into the nineteenth centuries.

General James Francis Edward Keith was born in Scotland in 1696, brother of the last Earl Marishal, and from a fervent Jacobite kindred. After fighting in the 1715 Jacobite rebellion, he first went to Spain and then entered the Russian military and had a distinguished career. The Empress Anna (d. 1740) allegedly declared that she would sooner lose 10,000 of her best soldiers than Keith. He was equally loyal to the Empress Elizabeth (who reigned 1741–62), perhaps overly so, since there was a story that the empress wished to marry him and he feared being sent to Siberia if he refused her. If that was true, he escaped that fate and managed to enter the service of Frederick the Great and die heroically at the Battle of Hochkirch in 1758.

Both Keith brothers and other exiled Jacobites were prominent freemasons, an affiliation that allowed important networking of like-minded Stuart supporters for many years. The Jacobite involvement in freemasonry, and especially its esoteric offshoot linked to the ideals of the medieval Knights Templar, is a fascinating branch of underground history, clouded until recent years because of the inherent secrecy in these networks, but also because of the insistence of some modern masons that these historical links did not exist. There was ongoing competition in the eighteenth century between masons associated with the Stuarts and those who supported the British establishment. Some within the British establishment suspiciously viewed masonic-Templar Jacobites as quasi pagans and played the anti-Semitic card because of supposedly Jewish cabalistic influence in their rival form of masonry, and because some British Jews abroad supported the Stuarts. The history of this masonic-Templar struggle has also been obscured by those who take a more occult view of the organisations involved and add a great deal of unsubstantiated material into the mix.

Prince Charles Edward was allegedly initiated into the masonic chapter of the Knights Templar at Holyrood in Edinburgh in 1746. Scotland had been the crucible of freemasonry in the seventeenth century and the movement was closely linked with the Stuarts. He also allegedly became the 'hidden' Grand Master of the Masonic Knights Templar, at the centre of a network that was initially Franco-Scottish but spread its influence to other nations. In contrast to the anaemic ideals of later masonic masons, the dynamic for the original lodges was the spread of free thinking through the integration of a number of concepts taken from ancient wisdom. And of course, on a secular level, it allowed Jacobites and their sympathisers in many nations to connect and exchange views. The Scottish-originated form of freemasonry was soon popular in Europe, spread not only by Scots but other Jacobites including Charles Radcliffe, Earl of Derwentwater.

Irishmen were also active in the overlapping worlds of freemasonry and Jacobitism, both in their own nation and in France, where they were instrumental in bringing the movement to prominence. An Irishman named Daniel d'Heguerty was responsible for encouraging the foundation of lodges all over France. The long tradition of Irish military identity in France helped to allow freemasonry to prosper in their adopted country. An Irish corps known as the Royal Irish, who became the Regiment of Walsh, stated that they had their own freemasonry unit as early as 1688, which came with them when they relocated to France. By 1772 it was still within their regiment and was known as the French lodge *Parfaite Égalité*. The masonic lodge in Bordeaux, which ironically termed itself 'Anglaise', was almost entirely an Irish club.

Although the Jacobite masonic network eventually foundered, its ideals lived on in several channels. One of the most interesting conduits for it was in the life of Lord George Gordon (1751–93), scion of an ancient Scottish house, who became a Jew, MP, Gaelic champion, advocate for freedom worldwide, and the general embodiment of an irritant to the English establishment. He was of course written off by mainstream history as a lunatic. Various Scottish masonic lodges and groups, mostly emanating from France, helped to spread the fraternity of Jacobite ideas throughout Europe. But these connections did not translate into any solid political momentum, or at least not enough to give the exiled Stuarts enough backing to ensure success in reconquering Great Britain. Some of the Jacobite exiles, exhausted by endless underground political intriguing in Europe, took further refuge in mysticism. In 1736, the chevalier Andrew Michael Ramsay (for a short time tutor to the Young Pretender) was planning on transforming Jacobite masonic lodges into a new knightly order that drew on the high traditions of the Knights Templar and Hospitaller. Though it has not been definitely proven that Prince Charles Edward Stuart remained actively involved in freemasonry, some contemporaries, like the Frenchman Lambert de Lintot, insisted that he was chief of a masonic sect named the Royal Order. Both the Frenchman Martinès de Pasqually and the German Karl Gotthelf von Hund claimed a link with the Young Pretender in this organisation, with the latter stating he had personally been initiated into freemasonry by the prince.

King Gustav III of Sweden was fascinated by Scottish freemasonry and contacted the ageing prince in Italy and elicited his support in exporting the rites and rituals of the organisation to his own realm. Prince Charles Edward happily agreed and sent a friendly missive to masons in Sweden:

> We Charles Edward, by the Grace of God, Sovereign Chief and Hereditary Grand Master of the Holy Order of the Knights of St. John of the Temple...last Prince and legitimate Heir of the Royal House of the Stuarts, to all those dear and respectable brothers who read the present letters patent, *Salut*.

According to Daniel Szechi, at this stage of his life, Charles Edward had sunk so low that he cynically took advantage of the masonic legend that he had been a masonic secret master and tried to con the Swedish monarch for the sake of eliciting some drinking money from him (which he then didn't receive). Both princes effectively cheated each other. The details of Prince Charles as the secret head of a shadowy order are frustratingly vague, and this aspect of his character together with his elusive nature has fed into a faint tradition of him somehow being an occult master. The later nineteenth-century writer John Goodrich in *The Light of the West* (1898) vaguely alluded to the prince possessing some Gnostic secret jewel after the Battle of Culloden. The nearest we have to any evidence of the declining Charles Edward taking an interest in any recondite knowledge is the rather wistful anecdote of him by an English Miss Miller, who spent an evening with him in 1775. The fallen prince showed her the illustrated *Tarrochi* cards he was amusing himself with – a form of tarot – and began to speak allusively of their meaning. But his English visitor was too reticent to let him explain their symbolic meaning.

Most of the elusive and dizzyingly diverse masonic and templar hives of exiled Stuart supporters vanished into the Jacobite mist long before the end of the eighteenth century. Even mundane, non-masonic Jacobites were keen to stay in the shadows and some have left little trace of their loyalties. So, it is hard to assess the involvement of senior members of the movement with any form of freemasonry. Some pseudo-secret organisations certainly involved the Jacobite monarchy, such as the mock chivalric Most Knightly Order del Toboso, whose international membership comprised upper-class Scottish, Irish and English Jacobites (including the omnipresent general George Keith, the Earl Marischal) and even had the Stuart princes as adolescent members. Despite this, it seems to have been more fraternal than political or mystical in nature. But the impressive networking organisation built up on the continent by Stuart-supporting masons was another unfortunate example of excellent intentions remaining unfulfilled in the long term and not used to its full potential.

Chapter 7

The Ghost and the Red Fox

On 8 November 1752, James Stewart of the Glens was hanged at Ballachulish in Argyll, found guilty of complicity in murder of the government factor Colin Campbell of Glenure the same year. Campbell, known by some as the Red Fox, was assassinated by a rifle shot by someone who was sympathetic to the pro-Jacobite families he was dispossessing and taking rents from as a state agent in the area. The actual killer was unknown but the trial blamed the Jacobite Alan Breck Stewart, later made famous in Robert Louis Stevenson's novel *Kidnapped* (1886). Blurred loyalties were alive and well in the district, to the detriment of justice, reflecting the fluid pattern of politics in Scotland at the time. James Stewart was related to the dispossessed Laird of Appin who had fled to France after Culloden, and he simultaneously acted as a sympathetic agent for him as being in the employ of the British government as an aide to Colin Campbell. The incorrigible Alan Stewart may have been a recalcitrant rebel, but he had earlier been an enlisted man who fought against the Jacobites. Alan Breck Stewart fled the country, probably to France, and the mists of legend obscured him. James Stewart of the Glens was executed for a crime that, in all probability, he had no active part.

Stewart's trial and execution can be correlated with that of Dr Archibald Cameron, who was hanged at Tyburn in London on 7 June 1753. A long-time and active Jacobite agent in Europe and Great Britain, Cameron's death also caused disquiet among those not overly sympathetic to the exiled Stuart monarchy. Cameron was – according to some – a pacifist participant only in the Jacobite army, being a medical doctor. There was no doubting his ardour, however, and personal attachment to Prince Charles Edward Stuart, to whom he was loyal right to the end. His own family, however, had deeply divided loyalties and he was likely betrayed to the British authorities by the Scottish agent known as 'Pickle the

Spy'. It might be argued that Great Britain was right to rid itself, less than a decade after Culloden, of these two prominent rebels and their deaths underlined once and for all the treacherous episode of the Jacobite rebellion. Yet neither man was a prominent combatant in rebel ranks and the element of official vindictiveness in both convictions seems evident.

The murder of the Red Fox has been relegated (or elevated) into one of the great historical mysteries of Scottish history. The true identity of the killer is said to have been handed down the generations of one family in the Appin district and never revealed, though there have been countless books and articles that have attempted to get to the truth of the incident. The motive for the murder at least appears to have been simple. The Appin Murder, as the incident was known, was a reprisal for Colin Campbell's prominent part in evicting Stewart tenants from their historical land holdings in the district. It was therefore linked to the more general series of evictions that swept across the western Highlands for several generations after the Jacobite revolution. The primary motive for the forced depopulation of settled communities was economic, with sheep farming being of greater value to landowners than the meagre revenue that subsistence tenant farmers provided them. But the impetus to effect this widespread change came with the breaking of the traditional Highland society that had existed for hundreds of years, and which was targeted by the British government after Culloden.

A complicating factor in the Appin Murder was the local rivalry between the Campbells and the Stewarts. While the former were pro-Hanoverian and acted for the British government, the Stewarts were mainly Jacobite by sympathy or action. Following the end of the '45, the commission for forfeited estates managed those lands that had been held by participants in the failed rebellion. In Argyll, these included Ardsheal, Callart and Mamore. Campbell collected rents on behalf of the government, though tenants in some cases still sent funds to the exiled Jacobite original owners who had fled abroad. Local feeling was further heightened when Campbell raised eviction actions against some tenants and sought to give his relatives the forfeited farms. Such an incendiary mixture of feelings and causes was bound to reach a crisis point. Campbell was not quite the Hanoverian ogre portrayed by his enemies and seems to have discharged his duties without undue malice. He was even censured by the Westminster authorities in 1751 when he was suspected of being too lenient on former Jacobites. It did not save him from death.

On 14 May 1752 Colin Campbell of Glenure was making his way along the coast of Argyll in the sheltering woods of Lettermore, in the company of his nephew Mungo Campbell and several others. The party were on their way to evict some Cameron tenants for non-payment of rent. They did not reach their destination. Two shots rang out from the hillside above the road. Colin Campbell fell from his horse, fatally wounded, and a figure in a dun-coloured coat was seen fleeing across the slope. He was never certainly identified beyond all shadow of doubt, but the subsequent trial declared that this assassin was Alan Breck Stewart, a notorious local figure who had been in the Jacobite ranks at Culloden and was now a soldier in Lord Ogilvy's regiment in the French army. Alan Breck was certainly in the locality and had been seen several times flaunting the price on his head by wearing his military uniform. Furthermore, he made no secret of his contempt for the government agent Colin Campbell. On one occasion he stated that he wished someone would make a 'blackcock' of the Red Fox; that is, slaughter him. Following the murder, Alan Stewart fled east into the Rannoch Moor area of Perthshire and his trail vanished, though he probably managed to board a ship and escape again to France. His only later, fleeting appearances will be examined later.

James Stewart had played a canny game with regard to Colin Campbell and, on the face of it, he accepted the status quo of dispossession of his friends and neighbours in an Argyll dominated by pro-government Campbell interests. Not only was he a paid underling of Campbell, he was usually on notably friendly terms with him, though on one drunken occasion the two men came close to blows. Alcohol may also have prompted James's unfortunately remembered statement 'that he would travel upon his knees to get a propper opportunitie of shooting Gleneur throw the head'. Stewart placidly accepted Campbell's insistence that he give up the tenancy of his own farm to make way for one of the Red Fox's associates. James Stewart was the illegitimate brother of Charles Stewart, Laird of Ardsheal, who had led his kinsmen throughout the Jacobite rebellion and had then escaped to France. Though Ardsheal's estates had been confiscated, his income as an exile in France was maintained by revenues given by his former tenants. James Stewart was, in effect, his agent and he was also close to Alan Breck Stewart. The latter had been fostered in his household and the two men maintained close relations. The wanted man had been in James's house around the time of the killing and had been assisted with clothing and money.

The trial of James Stewart was never going to be fair, given the necessity to bring someone to account for the murder of Campbell. The latter's clan were heavily represented in the jury (eleven men out of fifteen) and on the bench alongside two lords of justiciary was Archibald Campbell, 3rd Duke of Argyll. Due to the evidence, there was no chance that Stewart could be found guilty as being one of those who actually shot the victim. It was enough to show that he knew of the plot and was criminally complicit in the execution. Due process was followed in the proceedings and the jury did debate the verdict for a creditably decent time, but there was little doubt about the guilty outcome.

James of the Glen delivered a moving, half-hour speech before they hanged him, protesting his innocence. His corpse was chained up and hung on a gibbet on the spot and was guarded by soldiers. After the Duke of Argyll died in 1761, his successor, John Campbell, the 4th Duke, allowed the gibbet to be removed for decency's sake. He was spurred on when one of his tenants mentioned that he disliked seeing his neighbour so often, meaning the view of the rotting corpse he could view from his land. Stewart's bones were taken away and interred beside his wife. The action did something to heal the perennial hatred between the Stewarts and Campbells in this part of Argyll, an enmity that went some way beyond the transitory contest between Jacobites and Hanoverians for the mastery of Great Britain.

Was Alan Breck Stewart the assassin of the Red Fox? It seems likely he was involved in a possible local conspiracy to rid the district of this hapless man who was more hated for his role than personally. A closer look at him shows a more flawed and complex character than is sometimes portrayed. His pre-rebellion activities are obscure, though he is described in one document as having the mundane occupation of brewer. Perhaps because of economic reasons he joined the British army and was actually on active service when the Jacobite Rebellion broke out. It was said that he was in the ranks at the Battle of Prestonpans on 21 September 1745 and was so disconcerted at facing an enemy army that included associates from his old district that he soon afterwards deserted and joined the rebel Appin Regiment, comprised in large part of fellow Stewarts. There may be a suspicion that Alan was rather too conspicuous in the neighbourhood around the time of the murder, even to the extent of openly wearing his French army uniform. Added to this was public remarks against Campbell, plus casually spending part of the day of the murder choosing to fish in a place very near where the crime took place. Was Alan Breck Stewart setting himself up as a suspect while the real killers were quieter men who went about the business of death unnoticed in the locality and melted into the landscape again once the deed was done? No one will ever know, but this supposition is plausible. One theory says that he laid a false trail by fleeing from the scene and implicating himself in the crime, and that this was done deliberately and for a payment. It was said that the murder weapon – 'the black gun of misfortune' – was hidden for many years in a hollow tree near Ballachulish House. It was later displayed at nearby Dunstaffnage. As another aside, it is worth noting that the Duke of Cumberland, who believed that most Scots were rebels, expressed his opinion that the murdered Colin Campbell of Glenure, along with his half-brother Barcaldine, was a Jacobite. Another prominent Campbell, the Earl of Breadalbane, made sure these past associations were dampened down.

Like other anti-heroes, Alan Breck Stewart's actions and motives remain unresolved. He vanished from history after the incident. The trial of James Stewart certainly vilified Alan as a wastrel and a sponger; one witness stated that he had never known him to do a day's work. He had written from France to confess his own guilt and the accused man's innocence to save James Stewart. But it came too late, and it was not believed. Six years later a story says that he surprised a group of Argyll men serving with the British army in the wilds of Canada, wandering into their tent at night, wearing the uniform of a French officer. He claimed that the letter he had sent had merely been a ploy to free James of the Glen and said he had no part in the assassination. As a parting gift, he promised these countrymen he would arrange a breach in the circle of French troops around them. They duly escaped through a gap in the encirclement next day. There are doubts that the event happened. There was one more transitory view of him, or of a man who may have been him, described by Walter Scott in his notes to *Rob Roy* (1817). Around the year 1789, a Scottish tourist found himself in the Paris apartment of a Scottish Benedictine priest. He had been invited there because it had a view of a parade that was due to take place.

> He found, sitting by the fire, a tall, thin, raw-boned, grim-looking old man, with the petit croix of St Louis. His visage was strongly marked by the irregular projections of the cheek-bones and chin. His eyes were grey. His grizzled hair exhibited marks of having been red, and his complexion was weather-beaten, and remarkably freckled. Some civilities in French passed between the old man and my friend, in the course of which they talked of the streets and squares of Paris, till at length the old soldier, for such he seemed, and such he was, said with a sigh, in a sharp Highland accent, 'Deil ane o' them a' is worth the Hie street of Edinburgh!' On enquiry, this admirer of Auld Reekie, which he was never to see again, proved to be Alan Breck Stewart. He lived decently on his little pension, and had, in no subsequent period of his life, shown any thing of the savage mood, in which he is generally believed to have assassinated the enemy and oppressor, as he supposed him, of his family and clan.

Evocative and romantic as this strange meeting seems, there are doubts that the man was indeed the famous Highland renegade. For a start, the young Alan Breck was consistently described as having dark hair. James of the Glen (who may have believed him guilty of the murder) described him in a letter as 'a desparat foolish fellow...a tall pock-pitted lad' with 'very black hair'. The story that Alan Breck later fought against the British with the French army in North America is speculation, as is the tale that he inconspicuously chose to migrate to Ireland and spend his last days there on a farm.

Tradition and folklore pick the winners in history as well as any historian with their own agenda. The shots that killed Glenure reverberated in the district where the killing took place and the echo lives on still. In Appin, the murder was more than a historical whodunnit; it was an event that was woven into the identity of the area. When Robert Louis Stevenson came here in 1881, the locals were adamant that Alan Stewart was not the guilty party. He heard that the descendants of the real man who fired the fatal shot were still thriving in the locality, but nobody would name the perpetrator. Several decades earlier, the folklorist John Dewar collected surviving traditions about the murder and Campbell of Glenure here. The murdered man was firmly portrayed as a heartless villain. One local legend insisted that he had purposely shot a local woman while trying to pursue cattle thieves. Another tale insisted that he purposely slaughtered some minor criminals rather than take them prisoner. The reality of the situation in Appin in the district and the real-life character of the Red Fox was rather more nuanced in those divided days after Culloden. Almost a century after Stevenson, the writer George Malcom Thomson said he knew of one woman in the district who knew the name of the real murderer. 'A Stewart,' he said, 'would sooner tell you the story of why his brother had suddenly to flee the country last year than disclose the name of the man who fired the shot in Lettermore Wood in 1752.'

Alan Breck lingered on as the admittedly lovable rogue in Robert Louis Stevenson's novel *Kidnapped* (1886), though his literary persona seems to have been modelled partly on that more genuinely heroic Jacobite soldier John Roy Stuart. The events in the novel are set in a plausibly realistic post-Culloden Scottish setting, and Alan steals the limelight from the main protagonist David Balfour for much of the narrative and his enigmatic presence also makes several appearances in the sequel *Catriona* (1893). Stevenson's narrative notably gives an even-handed account of the Jacobite times, unlike Walter Scott's ultimately pro-Whig account in *Waverley*.

If the murder of Colin Campbell and execution of James Stewart have reverberated down the years because of the injustice, another event around the time has left a stranger resonance. The supernatural associations of the Jacobite cause were deeply woven into the fabric of Scottish Highland folklore and because of this they have been disregarded as a legitimate part of the study of the Jacobites. For some people, the supernatural and folklore belong in the same relegated cultural department as the sentimental nostalgia for the lost cause represented in saccharine ballads and verse. But the unseen world was very much alive in the eighteenth century and played its own part in the uprising.

Even as the conflict raged between government and Stuart forces, the balance of power was being divined by some in the Highlands. An eighteenth-century traveller, Thomas Pennant, says that a common soldier tried to foretell the result of the conflict between Stuart and Hanoverian by the use of an animal's shoulder blade, an ancient means of foretelling the future, known as *slinneannachd* at the time of Culloden. A pseudonymous writer called Theophilus, who published a book in 1763, wrote about the endemic use of second sight in the north of Scotland. Even before the '45 uprising began there were signs of the future upheaval. A servant in Benbecula, in the year 1744, suddenly had a vision of British soldiers invading the island, which came to pass during the Jacobite incursion. A fleet of phantom warships was seen off Mull and Tiree and spectral armies were seen fighting in the sky in Lochaber. A loch in Skye turned the colour of blood.

The prerogative of seeing future events concerning the civil war was not restricted to those who supported the Jacobites or were indifferent to either side. Duncan Forbes of Culloden, lord president of Scotland, a supporter of the British government, supposedly had a clairvoyant vision about the future shortly after the Battle of Prestonpans in 1745. He looked from his window at Culloden House onto the moor that would be the scene of a battle seven months later and declared, 'Depend upon it, all the disturbances will be determined on this spot.' A clergyman from Skye also wrote of various strange visions associated with the then current Jacobite insurrection. Most remarkable was the range of visions afflicting John Ferguson, a seer and natural wonder who had survived on only water for several years. Ferguson saw waking dreams of local men from Argyll before they joined the Jacobites, and his dreams foretold doom. More intriguingly, he had strange hallucinations of a young man, at first hunting with greyhounds. A following vision had the youth trying to catch a ponderous bubble above his head, which then fell and crushed him. The third vision of this figure showed the young man dolefully dressed in black, being led to a block by several people, 'whereon his Head was laid, and then chopp'd off with a Hatchet'. After careful questioning, he ascertained by the description of this young man that it was Charles Edward Stuart, the Young Pretender. But, of course, the executioner never got to him. Hanoverian wish fulfilment seemed to be the basis of this seer's second sight. On the other hand, there were pro-Jacobite visions. John Prebble related that a strange vision in the sky two years after Culloden rewrote history in a heavenly fashion and showed a Jacobite army returning to overwhelm the Hanoverian British forces. In Aberdeen eleven men and women swore that they saw a phantom battle in the sky between an army bearing a Scottish flag and another bearing a British one. The latter beat back the Scots one twice, but in the end the latter won and the dreamscape vanished forever. The famous seventeenth-century Highland prophet known as the Brahan Seer is supposed to have foretold the massive seismic misery that Culloden would cause in the Highlands:

> Oh Drummossie, thy bleak moor shall, ere many generations have passed, be stained with the best blood of the Highlands. Glad I am that I will not see that day, for it will be a fearful time; heads will be lopped off by the score, and no mercy shown on either side.

Even those who disparage the mechanism of second sight might recognise the psychological imperative behind the urge to use otherworldly means to ascertain the future. A self-satisfied London alderman may not have felt the necessity to have recourse to divination, but an impoverished Morayshire peasant faced with personal and cultural extinction would have been less complacent and turned to different sources of information about the future.

The supernatural association with the cause of the royal Stuart family was powerfully evident during the time of the 1745 uprising. When the Young Pretender announced that he had come home when he approached the coast of Scotland, the identification between his blood and the land was of profound significance to some supporters. Seton Gordon tells the tradition of a boulder named *A' Chlach Sgoilte*, the Split Stone, which is said to have spontaneously split from top to bottom on the day of the Battle of Culloden. Local people knew what this natural omen signified. A Stewart woman whose husband was fighting that day for the righteous cause exclaimed, 'The cause of the prince is lost, and I myself am a widow.' She was not quite right, for Charles Edward in the fugitive weeks ahead became almost the embodiment of the spirit of Scotland.

One otherworldly event became nearly as celebrated as the Appin case and also involved a judicial element. On 28 September 1749 an English sergeant in Guise's regiment, Arthur Davies, was travelling between two military stations in the central Highlands when he was murdered. The trial of the two men accused of his death took place in Edinburgh in June 1754. The accused were Duncan Terig or Clark and Alexander Bain MacDonald. Post-Culloden, Davies had been one of those soldiers enforcing the peace in formerly hostile Jacobite territory. He had been in charge of a group of eight soldiers, called a *piquet*, at a small farm outpost near Inverey, Aberdeenshire. The sergeant was a conspicuous figure who gained attention because of his appearance: he wore gold rings and had silver buckles on his shoes as well as a silver watch. It was also known that Davies had a purse of fifteen guineas or more that he used to carry around with him – a tempting target. On the September day of his disappearance, he set out with four soldiers to rendezvous with another military party at Glenshee. On the way, Davies parted company with his patrol. He was a keen hunter and wanted to pursue some game, saying he would catch up with his men later. His party returned home from Glenshee without meeting their leader. However, he did turn up at Glenshee, where he was cautioned about returning to his own base alone. He dismissed the remark and said he was not afraid because he was armed. That was the last time anyone saw him alive. A search was made for the soldier but no body was found. But his ghost was seen in the lonely glen. It disappeared when people approached it.

The following summer Donald Farquharson, who had known the sergeant, was approached by Alexander MacPherson who claimed that he had been visited by the ghost. The first appearance came when he was in bed and the figure was wearing a blue coat and announced his identity. When the terrified man refused to heed the vision, it came back another night naked and implored MacPherson to tell Farquharson, and it would then inform them where its body lay and begged for its bones to be buried. Farquharson was understandably dubious, but the other man's employer had also seen the naked figure of the Englishman. He accompanied MacPherson to the Hill of Christie at the head of Glenconie where they found remains. The man had been shot and he wore the remains of a blue coat, but his gold and silver were gone. With him there was a hat marked with his initials ARD. They buried the remains on the spot.

Meanwhile it was rumoured that a previously poor man named Duncan Terig was now conspicuously wealthy enough to stock two farms and his wife was wearing two rings that looked like the sergeant's. He was arrested along with Alexander MacDonald, and the men were found in possession of the other rings and some of his silver buttons. Some of their relatives implicated them that they had been seen in the murder area. They went on trial at the High Court of Justiciary in Edinburgh on 10 June 1754.

During the proceedings there was widespread scepticism about the circumstances and the defence counsel pertinently enquired of MacPherson which language the supposed sergeant had spoken to him in. 'As good Gaelic as I ever heard in Lochaber,' was the reply. 'Pretty well for the ghost of an English sergeant,' the lawyer commented. It was ascertained that Davies could indeed only speak in his native language. The case naturally collapsed despite the weight of circumstantial evidence against the accused. Simple robbery and murder, anti-English outrage, or Jacobite act of revenge against an occupying enemy; it is anyone's guess.

There had been other sporadic instances of violence involving soldiers and natives after Culloden. In retaliation for an army attack in Lochgarry in July 1746, two hapless soldiers who were fishing in a loch were murdered and dismembered, probably by men from the Clan Cameron. On 27 May 1747 a man who had collaborated with the British army was dragged from his bed in Cullen, Aberdeenshire, and brutally slain. At the end of that August, Captain George Munro of Culcairn was murdered near Loch Arkaig. On the same day, a Whig laird named Alexander Garden was kidnapped in Banffshire. A £2,000 ransom was demanded, and paid, and no culprits were caught, though it was said the supposed ringleader said the money was little compensation for those people locally who had had their houses burnt by British soldiers. Even without the supernatural elements, these events formed an unsettling epilogue to the collapse of Jacobitism in Scotland. Sergeant Davies appears to be a hapless victim, albeit his gaudy wealth made him an easy target in a poverty-stricken district. The last of these deaths to consider is that of Dr Archibald Cameron, the last state-executed Jacobite in Great Britain.

Chapter 8

Dr Cameron and The Elibank Plot

If the trial and death of James Stewart of the Glens was a tragedy, it was matched by the death of Dr Archibald Cameron, a figure whose legend provides a low-key contrast to more conspicuous military Jacobite icons. The two judicial executions, one in Argyll and the other in London, happened within a year of each other and symbolised the brutal finality with which the Whig-ruled British state chose to deal with the Jacobite uprising.

If ever there was a widely lamented secular saint for the Jacobite cause in Scotland, it was Dr Cameron. And, like many saints, he was a controversial figure beneath the surface. Some part of his role in the fate of the mysterious Loch Arkaig treasure has already been examined. Despite the outpouring of outrage surrounding his death, Cameron is not as well-known as other Jacobite figures and yet his demise effectively marked the end of the political wing of the Jacobite endeavour. The immediate reaction to his end, in his native Highlands, is as a heroic and tragic fallen hero. The Gaelic poet John Cameron of Dochanassie eulogised him in verse:

> Last night I lay dreaming
> what I'd sooner see waking,
> that thou, O Gill' Easbuig,
> hadst come to succour thy country;
> but when I awakened out of my vision,
> I could not find thee near me,
> thou wast far from thy country.

But in the years after his death, Cameron's fate faded away in popular memory, just one more bitter memory connected with the failed Jacobite rebellion. The Highlands were more concerned with a rearguard action to save their language and culture; lamenting for an individual sacrificed for a long-gone royal family soon became a minor concern.

Supporters of Cameron made much of his honourable career and aspirations. Born the sixth child of John Cameron, eighteenth chief of Lochiel, in 1707, he was from a highly respected Jacobite kindred. His father John was an ardent Jacobite who had been exiled after his part in the 1715 Jacobite uprising. But there were signs that he was different from the usual *duine uasal*, or Highland gentleman. As the son of the clan chief, he was expected to find a career but he deviated from the legal profession he was earmarked for and chose to become a doctor. Archibald became a quietly respectable figure in his native community after studying medicine in Scotland and abroad, with no aspirations beyond helping his own small community. Another note of difference in him was his strong reluctance to follow his family's hereditary allegiance to the Stuart royal house. More than that, he foresaw the grave dangers of an uprising in the north that was improperly planned and without professional foreign support. Dr Archibald had deep reservations about challenging the British government and is said to have begged his brother on his knees not to be so foolhardy as to join the rebellion. Many of his kindred also had concerns about the wisdom of risking everything for the dubious cause of the young prince.

When the Young Pretender landed in Scotland, Cameron was sent by his brother Donald, met the Young Pretender and tried to dissuade him from continuing the rebellion, Donald possibly fearing that he would be turned from his convictions by the personal magnetism of the prince. Archibald Cameron held firm initially to his family's conviction that an unplanned insurrection at that moment would be disastrous. In the royal presence, the doctor 'talked a lot and promised nothing'. This talent for dissembling was a trait that may have helped him later in his covert activities. But Charles Edward still attempted to convert him and brought the full force of his personality to bear on the doctor, who was forced to admit, with a touch of dark foresight, that should he side with the prince, he would be the last to leave it. Still, Prince Charles Edward upbraided Donald Cameron of Lochiel for breaking his word since he had apparently earlier promised to support the Jacobite cause.

Stung by this challenge to his pride and naturally swayed when the prince came to see him in person, Donald Cameron pledged his loyalty. By his authority as acting clan chief (his father was still exiled in Paris), he immediately raised 1,200 men of his clan and his brother was swept up in his tumultuous decision. Even at this stage, the doctor desperately resisted the decision. When Donald summoned him to a rendezvous in preparation for raising the clan for the cause, Archibald refused to appear and only showed signs of doubt when his brother beseeched him. Dr Cameron even begged his brother on his bended knees not to join the Jacobites. Archibald was not fully convinced that the cause merited the enormous risk. The young chief's wife tried to appeal to him without success and it was said that Donald Cameron threatened to pistol whip Archibald into changing his mind. But eventually Archibald relented, though he refused any commission in the Jacobite army. He diligently served as a doctor in the campaign, tending to Jacobite troops and captured Hanoverian soldiers alike. At the Battle of Falkirk he tended his injured brother until he was wounded in the leg himself. Following Culloden, the doctor spent some time with the prince, advising him on the best places to conceal himself in the countryside. He was undoubtedly one of the leading Jacobites present when a load of French gold was landed in the western Highlands and concealed near Loch Arkaig. Although his association with the fate of this treasure is unclear, the fact that he was involved made him a prime person of interest afterwards for the British state.

The Cameron brothers spent some time undercover in the Western Isles and soon afterwards escaped into exile in France. Archibald became physician in a regiment commanded by his brother, then joined Ogilvy's REGIMENT before going to Flanders. If he had confined himself to these activities, he may have enjoyed a safer future. But it is clear that he continued to be actively involved in the Jacobite cause. Following his brother's death and lack of promised funds from a Spanish commission, he appealed to the Old Pretender in Rome for assistance, without success. Partly motivated perhaps by necessity, he returned to Scotland, ostensibly to raise funds for poor Jacobite exiles in Europe but it seems certain he was also agitating for the Jacobite cause, acting under a commission from Charles Edward to bolster support for another insurrection in Scotland. It was also said that he intrigued with Frederick of Prussia in an attempt to gain troops for another Jacobite invasion. Cameron was instructed to make contact with that recalcitrant Jacobite fugitive Cluny Macpherson and make every attempt to recover the lost Jacobite treasure. Despite being accused of stealing £6,000 of the gold by the notorious double agent Glengarry, there was no actual proof that Dr Cameron misappropriated any of the legendary funds, but he may well have been motivated by personal poverty to claim what he saw as his and his family's appropriate expenses from the treasure. The evidence suggested that he acted honourably in the matter and, with slightly less probability, in his supposed involvement in the plot to assassinate King George II and other Hanoverian royals.

Whatever the truth, Cameron was captured and brought first to Edinburgh and then transported to London. He revealed nothing significant during questioning, even when he was brought before the Privy Council. Following a trial, he was sentenced to be hanged, taken down when still alive, then having his bowels removed, his body quartered and finally decapitated. Efforts were made by the Jacobite leadership abroad, and others, to have his life spared. But appeals for clemency on the basis that he held commission under foreign powers came to nothing. Even his wife tried to appeal for clemency with the government, but it came to nothing. His body was cut down after twenty minutes hanging and his heart was removed and burned. If he had been a priest rather than a doctor, Cameron would undoubtedly have been held up as a true martyr.

The extent to which Archibald was an active supporter of the Jacobites during the uprising, albeit he was not an actual soldier, deserves consideration. He is said to have acted as a willing local guide to the prince during his early days in Scotland finding his bearings. He was also a key player in the concealment of the Loch Arkaig trove of gold landed in Scotland in 1746. Pro and con propaganda material wove a concealment around the legend of Dr Cameron. His many supporters cited instances of his humanity to people in his community and beyond.

During the uprising he is said to have saved the inhabitants of the town of Kirkintulloch from massacre after two Jacobite Camerons were killed there. He also reportedly prevented the execution of government prisoners by fellow Jacobites after the Battle of Prestonpans on 21 September 1745. When the Jacobites were retreating from England and came to Kendal in Cumberland, he supported the townsfolk against a hefty cash levy that Jacobite officials tried to extort from them. Again, we hear of him as the moderate voice of reason when some on his side wanted to attack the house of their enemy, Campbell of Invera, and he persuaded them otherwise.

Dr Cameron's wife, Jean Cameron of Dungannon, bore the brunt of his ill fate. She was repulsed three times from the presence of the king and other royals in a desperate attempt to have him pardoned while he was imprisoned in London and her health declined perilously. She was even confined herself at one stage and was deprived of the chance of seeing her husband during his final days. Even before this, in the time after Culloden, she suffered great hardship along with many Highland families. When her husband was hiding from government troops for several months after the defeat, two of Jean Cameron's children died. She was advised not to bury them in the family vault for fear that someone would disinter them to steal their linen shrouds. Another of her daughters was stripped by government troops.

Beyond the competing propaganda pen pictures of Cameron – either a martyr or a traitor – there are few intimate glimpses of the actual man. Before the Jacobite war his eldest brother Donald wrote to his cousin with an assessment of his sibling: 'My brother Archie has capacity enough but no application,' and suggests that he rather drifted into medicine without having a burning calling towards the profession. Such an observation may suggest that he fell into Jacobitism, as well as medicine, almost by default. Many of the voices raised against him were biased supporters of the British state, but there were others among his own people that were equally damning.

One such was a prisoner named John Cameron, who testified that Dr Cameron came to another fellow clansman, Cameron of Dungannon, 'and forcibly brought from thence five hundred men, most of the name of

Cameron, threatening them if they did not come directly he would burn their houses and cut them in pieces'. Another member of the same clan averred, less dramatically, that the doctor 'killed four of my cows before he consented to go with him'. The first incident happened soon after Dr Cameron's reluctant conversion to the Jacobite cause. If it happened, it possibly signifies some displaced anger arising from his own situation, or else perhaps was an overt act of aggression designed to show his brother and other strong pro-Jacobites that he really was committed to their course of action. Forced participation in the Jacobite army during the '45, through intimidation of clan leaders and lairds, was not uncommon.

Though he died declaring his loyalty to the royal house of Stuart, there is some evidence that he wavered before his day of reckoning. Nathaniel Carrington was a messenger who witnessed a conversation between the doomed Cameron and lieutenant of the Tower of London, in which the desperate prisoner assured the gaoler that, if his life was spared, 'He would engage to be made anyways usefull, And do any Service'. His turncoat proposal, if it is true, was turned down by authorities who were unconvinced by his volte-face. In the aftermath of his arrest, Charles Edward in Europe was rightfully fearful that his captors would break Cameron and took extensive measures to cover his tracks and destroy incriminating documentation.

Like other prominent Jacobites who suffered from the cynical indignity of a state trial in London, Dr Cameron accepted his fate calmly, being dragged through the streets of London to his execution place at Tyburn on a sled. He nodded at those people he knew in passing, as if he was on a leisurely carriage drive, and remarked to the clergyman who attended him at the end that it was a glorious day and his new birthday. There were more witnesses there at this birthday than at his first. He was left hanging for some time and then his heart was removed and burnt, but he was spared the agonies of drawing and quartering.

Barring his brave death, Archibald Cameron was hardly the atypical dashing military hero who gladly forfeited his life for the house of Stuart. ''Twas thy boldness that destroyed thee,' claimed the elegy by Cameron of Dochanassie, but this was not quite the case. His undoubted bravery shone most when he returned to Scotland and worked hard to rekindle the lost flame of support for the Stuarts that had been recently snuffed out. He must have known that he was taking a terrible risk in a country swarming with military. In the end, if his loyalty did waver in his final days, he hardly put himself in the same bracket as men like Lord Lovat who also died bravely, but who was a towering figure of notoriety.

Cameron wrote a statement justifying his loyalty to the Stuarts on a few scraps of paper in the Tower. He condemned the already notorious atrocities of the Butcher Cumberland. He also condemned the judge and gently taunted the lack of proof of involvement in plotting against the crown:

> To cover the Cruelty of murdering me at this Distance of Time, from the passing of the *unjust Attainder*, I am accused of being deeply engaged in a *new plot* against this Government; which, if I was, neither the Fear of the worst Death their Malice could invent, nor much less the *blustering and noisy Threatnings of the tumultuous Council*, nor even their flattering Promises, could extort any Discovery of it from me; yet not so much as one Evidence was ever produced to make good the Charge.

Cameron was alluding to the Elibank Plot, the last semi-credible scheme of the Jacobites to regain power in Great Britain that came several years after the Battle of Culloden. Where the 1745 uprising was a stirring and bold military adventure, the Elibank affair of 1752–53 was a series of underground plots that were conducted in great secrecy. It could be argued also that this conspiracy which aimed, in one variation, at the assassination of the Hanoverian royal family, represented the moral decay of Jacobite ideals from its former conceptual height as a movement that derived some of its authority from the ideal of God-given royal power. The plot was more a series of tenuously related schemes that focused on seizing power in London. Due to the fragmentary nature of the evidence, getting to the truth of the main plot is hard to fathom.

One of the spurs for the plot was the sudden and unexpected visit of Prince Charles Edward Stuart to London in 1750. This appearance was made behind the backs of the prince's father and his brother Henry, as well as most of the Jacobite establishment in exile. Most of the prince's supporters in England were equally unaware that he was coming. One day in September, in her house in London, Lady Primrose was playing cards and looked up to see the Young Pretender enter the room. She carried on with her game despite her astonishment in order not to alert those present who had Hanoverian sympathies. The London visit only lasted for five days, but there were clandestine meetings held during this time, particularly one with the Duke of Beaufort and the Earl of Westmorland. Charles Edward was sizing up the possibility of making another daring attempt to recover his family's throne. It was during this trip that he converted to Anglicanism, a religious move that was much too late to convince those Catholic-hating opponents of the Stuarts; it also alienated long-suffering loyal Catholic Jacobites.

The Young Pretender himself may have been actively planning another invasion at this time since there is a record of his trying to buy a large number of firearms in Europe. The plan seems to have involved a landing of forces somewhere in northern England or Wales. There were rumours that a major European power, probably Prussia, was getting ready to support another Jacobite attempt at the British crown. Be that as it may, it was later said that a rather wilder plot was being engineered at the time or not long afterwards. One version of this plot was given by Lord Elcho, the former Jacobite soldier who allegedly cursed the fleeing Young Pretender on the field of Culloden. According to him, a young Scot named Alexander Murray, brother of Lord Elibank, forged a plan to have a group of sixty men attack the royal residence in London and either kidnap or assassinate the current royal family. As soon as this was accomplished, the prince was to hurry across the North Sea and seize power. Several English noblemen were privy to the plot.

Key players in the plot, according to Elcho, were a Lieutenant Colonel Macdonald and Dr Archibald Cameron. There is no proof of Cameron's active involvement in any of the London schemes; he may have been more involved in parallel projects in the far north. Scottish officers from Ogilvy's Regiment in France were also said to have been placed in London as co-ordinators of the enterprise. Other sources have vehemently denied that the prince would countenance the executions of the Hanoverian royal family and this seems accurate. However, the whole scheme, or the loose threads of plot and sub-plot are woven into a strange gossamer mesh of rumour. Some warning of renewed Jacobite intrigue was fed back to London by the Jacobite traitor known by the codename Pickle (Alastair Ruadh Mac Donell of Glengarry). He stated that a Swedish-backed force was preparing to invade Scotland and, at the same time, there were moves to plant 2,000–3,000 agents in London, ready to take the capital. The first move would have been to storm the royal residence, St James's Palace, and the date fixed for the event was 10 November 1752 (though alternative dates had been proposed in May or June 1753).

Another source states that Charles Edward was in the thick of some plans with a one-armed Irish military conspirator named Segrave that involved an idea to use an Irish group to kidnap the royal family and carry them into captivity overseas. Segrave had met with Charles Edward some time before 1752 and formulated an idea to have an Irish gang kidnap George II from his coach during one of his regular late-night excursions back from the theatre. It was confidently assumed the kidnap could be accomplished in ten minutes, after which the king would be spirited away to France. Charles Edward was adamant that no physical harm should befall his opponent, something he reiterated. The idea of kidnap was bandied about again several years later and was one of the possible schemes at the time of the Elibank plot.

In 1752, some Prussian support was again sought, but Frederick the Great followed the pattern of other supposedly sympathetic European monarchs and failed to provide the Jacobites any substantial material support. Frederick's Scottish confederate George Keith, the Earl Marischal, although a supporter of the Stuart cause, was personally doubtful about Prince Charles Edward and may have ensured that no real support was given, although his brother may have been involved to some extent in invasion negotiations. The exiled prince and his associates were involved in frenetic associations with all manner of potential allies and backers in Europe, plus other possible supporters such as plantation owners from the Caribbean. However, all the activity came to nothing. Wishful thinking and outright make belief were prominent elements in the plotting.

The kidnap scheme was supposedly minutely planned. As well as Ogilvy's Scots and Segrave's Irish, it was hoped that as many as 2,500 conspirators would be waiting in various places ready to support the coup, and that a large number of aldermen in London would spontaneously jump aboard the Jacobite bandwagon along with enough disaffected officers in the British military to ensure success. Murray's proposals were never followed through. Perhaps his co-conspirators baulked at his suggestion that it would be logistically more practical to kill the entire royal family rather than transport them abroad. It has also been suggested that he lost his nerve about the venture and then went abroad. Lack of support, from English Jacobites as well as European supporters, plus the perennial disunity and undermining activity from British spies, fatally destroyed the viability of the scheme. Paranoia was endemic in the ranks of the Stuart supporters, with some of them convinced (without reason) that the prince's hapless lover Clementina Walkinshaw was an agent for the British state. After the plot fizzled out, Murray remained abroad for nearly two decades but was able to return to Britain where he died, surprisingly untroubled by Hanoverian reprisals, at Taplow in Buckinghamshire in 1778.

Dr Archibald Cameron, as observed, had unproven involvement in the plotting. He certainly met the prince and then travelled to Scotland before the proposed coup to co-ordinate Jacobite support, but whether he had been made privy to the darker machinations that centred around London is unknown. His primary mission in the north was to reassemble clan support for another proposed uprising and probably attempt to find out the whereabouts of what remained of the Loch Arkaig gold. The government were quickly on his trail. He narrowly evaded capture by a troop of soldiers; his associate Lochgarry also evaded a trap set for him by the military. Cameron was eventually arrested on 20 March 1753, betrayed by others, and executed less than three months later. It is fairly certain too that his demise ended other serious Jacobite plans to stage further action in Great Britain.

Yet there was evidence of other elements of planning aimed at invasion. A huge store of weapons was ready to be sent to Scotland for distribution to awaiting rebels there. In 1753, leading Irish Stuart supporters assured

1. General Hugh Mercer. *Nova Scotia Historical Society*, 1912.

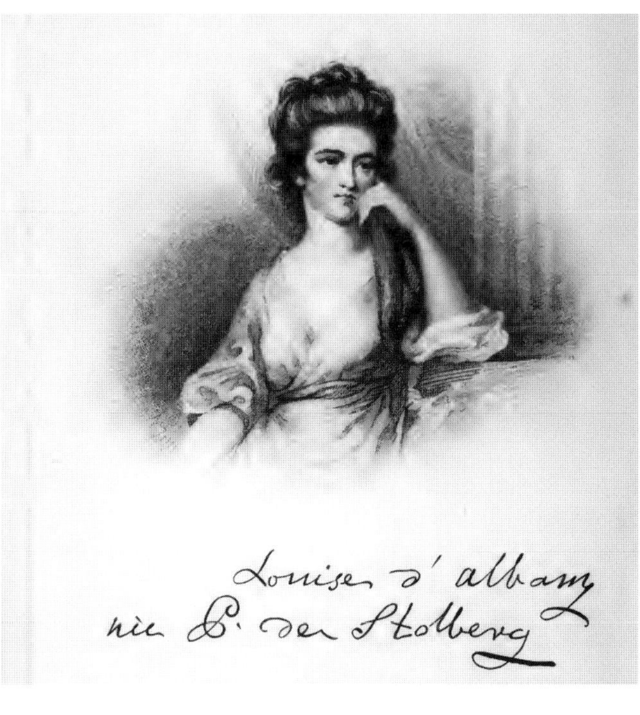

2. Princess Louisa, wife of Prince Charles Edward Stuart. *The Last Stuart Queen*, Herbert M. Vaughan, London, 1910.

3. Medal of Prince Charles Edward, 1772. *The Last Stuart Queen*, Herbert M. Vaughan, London, 1910.

4. The Stuart Palace in Florence. *The Last Stuart Queen*, Herbert M. Vaughan, London, 1910.

5. The Young Pretender in old age. *The Last Stuart Queen*, Herbert M. Vaughan, London, 1910.

6. Henry Stuart, Cardinal Duke of York. *The Last Stuart Queen*, Herbert M. Vaughan, London, 1910.

7. Prince Charles Edward, 1735. *Pickle the Spy*, London, 1897.

8. Charles and Henry Stuart. *The Companions of Pickle*, Andrew Lang, London, 1898.

9. Clementina Walkinshaw. *The Last of the Stuarts*, Henry Stuart, Cardinal of York, Herbert M. Vaughan, New York, 1906.

10. Lord Lovat's ghost. Eighteenth-century cartoon.

11. The royal Stuart monument in Rome. *The Last of the Stuarts, Henry Stuart, Cardinal of York*, Herbert M. Vaughan, New York, 1906.

12. Charles Edward Stuart Sobieski.

13. Jacobite image of the Duke of Cumberland.

14. The Royal House of Stuart Exhibition programme.

15. Crown Prince Rupprecht of Bavaria.

16. Theodore Napier.

17. James Butler, Duke of Ormond. *The Pretenders and their Adherents*, George Heneage Jess, London, 1901.

18. Regiment of Hibernia in Spanish service.

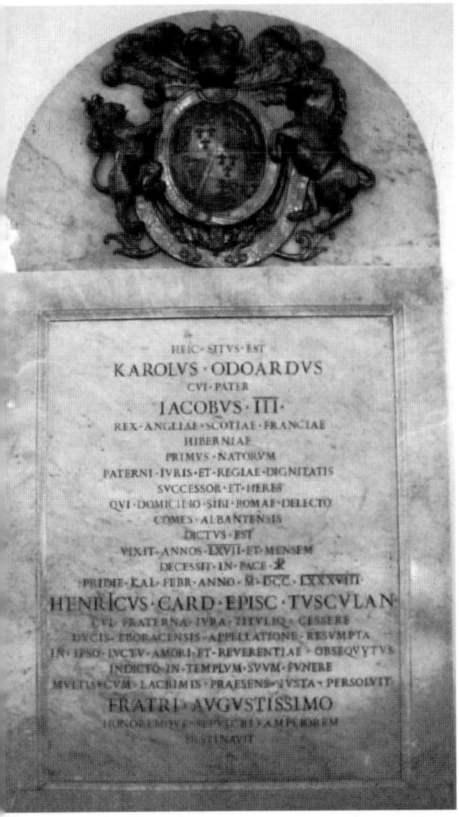

19. Monument to Charles Edward Stuart in Frascati Cathedral.

20. David Wemyss, Lord Elcho, in 1741. Painting at Gosford, from *A Short Account of the Affairs of Scotland*, Lord Elcho, Edinburgh, 1907.

21. *Kidnapped* film, 1917.

22. Simon, Lord Lovat. Drawing after William Hogarth.

leaders in France that they could readily raise 14,000 men whom they had in readiness of a dual attack in Argyll and in Wales. Viscount Clare, a commander of the Irish Brigade in France, was willing to send soldiers to participate in this manoeuvre. Such a double-pronged attack, perhaps combined with action in London, would have severely stretched British military resources. As it was, government spies were aware of the broad details of the plans.

As for the Young Pretender, he must have seen that the time was not ripe for another attempt at conquering his birthright. It never would be again. Prussia had let him down, just as France had done more than once in the past. Along with his leading supporters, he must have known that there was a traitor in his camp. Apart from the repulsive treachery of Pickle, there were numerous infiltrators and spies who could report on the activities of the Jacobites to the British government. For all their long experience in intrigue, the Stuarts' supporters were no match for the adept intelligence network developed by the British establishment.

Despite the failure of Elibank, there were a few final flickers of possibility around possible plans for another Jacobite invasion. Some eternally inventive exiles came up with ideas about how best to invade Britain, but most of these were dismissed by Prince Charles. He had no enthusiasm in any plot that would have the initial thrust against the Scottish Highlands, which he saw as being too practically remote from the British centre of power. On the other hand, his favoured option of striking directly at London was hampered by the continued lukewarm attitude of the English Jacobites. If he had reservations there, he was also suspicious about the renewed interest by the French in supporting his cause. He had been badly bitten by insufficient French support before and bitterly realised that they only wanted to play the Jacobite hand to backfoot British interests both in Europe and in North America. Over several years, he scornfully rejected personal participation in French military raids in both Majorca and America. French support for an actual landing in England was a more tantalising prospect. Ministers in France were divided about again supporting the deposed royal house. One scheme they put to the prince was for him to have support in retaking just Ireland

and Scotland, on the basis that they sought to divide and permanently weaken British power. This was naturally rejected by the prince.

Negotiations dragged on with France and hopeful feelers were sent out by the Jacobites to other apparently friendly powers: Austria, Sweden, France. But one major stumbling block to progress was that the Jacobites were divided into two blocks. Prince Charles Edward led the more dynamic, scheming group of Jacobites intent on recapturing Britain, while his father in Rome was resigned to his religious life and did not countenance any restoration at this date. Charles Edward Stuart was still straining every sinew, in vain, to retrench the Jacobite effort and gain support from the ruling powers on the continent. But the requisite pieces of fate did not come together in his favour. The nail in the coffin of Jacobite hopes forever was the devastating defeat of the French fleet at the Battle of Quiberon Bay on 24 and 25 November 1759. Had the result been reversed, France may have invaded Great Britain and the old Stuart dynasty dusted down and sent back to their ancestral homeland. The French military fell to a low ebb; the national economy was in tatters. Plans to help the deposed Stuart regime were shelved once and for all. The humiliating Peace of Paris in 1763 put an end to any further elaborate geopolitical scheming and made it clear that the Jacobites had no useful friends in France.

Chapter 9
The Jacobites and America

The American Revolution happened so soon after the Jacobite uprising in Great Britain that there were inevitably individuals involved in both momentous events. But, between the Jacobite defeat of 1746 and the beginning of the rebellion in America in 1765, the geopolitical landscape in the world had drastically altered. The significance of Jacobite efforts to restore the Stuarts to the British throne had changed from being a minor side line in European history to being a total irrelevance on the world stage.

Some Scottish Jacobites who had fought for the Stuarts and found their way to the New World were largely now ardently loyal to the British cause. And many of these emigrants had taken explicit oaths of loyalty, sometimes as the price for freedom, to the British state. Many instinctively recognised that the fight for the old Stuart cause was finished and reality made them cautious in espousing any further political uprising. Large numbers of these empire loyalists became displaced losers in the American Revolution and migrated north into what became Canada, and many of these were Highlanders. For many Gaels, North America was *Tìr a' Gheallaidh,* the Promised Land, and they saw no reason to jeopardise their place in paradise for the ideals of another group of disaffected rebels whose dispute with the colonial status quo seemed remote from their daily concerns.

A large number of Scots who served in a professional military capacity in North America were serving in fledgling Highland regiments and were the first generation of a remarkable military cadre that would have been unthinkable several decades previously. Large-scale recruitment from Highland clans into the British military was the ingenious concept of secretary of state William Pitt in the mid-1750s and fostered by the Duke of Argyll and others. Not only was it an ideal suggestion for fighting manpower for the empire's colonial efforts in the Seven Years' War and other theatres, it also effectively neutralised the latent threat of a rootless male population in the Highlands demoralised after the defeat of the Jacobites. It was not unknown, though likely it was uncommon, for former active Jacobite fighters to serve in a military capacity in the New World. Such men would have had disparate motives for bearing arms again, mostly defending their land and property. Former Jacobite Malcolm Macpherson justified allegiance to the crown during the Seven Years' War because he had 'a desire of being revenged on the French for their treacherous promises in 1745'.

Later, during America's struggle for independence, the scale of Scottish and particularly Highland loyalty to the British loyalist cause surprised many Englishmen. Six Highland regiments had been raised in Britain between 1756 and 1763. Around 12,000 men from the region took part in the Seven Years' War. The French in the New World gave the Highland troops the back-handed designation of *sauvages d'Écosse*, in respect of their military ferocity and uncivilised character. In America, one estimate states that as many as 90 per cent of loyalists recruited into the British army in America between 1775 and 1776 were Scottish, many of them Highland veterans. (Another evaluation says that 25 per cent of British troops in America from 1756 to 1775 were Scottish.) Virginia loyalists were strongly Scottish in composition and Georgia later banned Highlanders from settling there unless they had served the American cause. But there was some sympathy with the American cause even among the Highland regiments in Scotland, perhaps a feeling of kinship inspired by Culloden or their own threatened culture. Sixty men from the 71st Highlanders actually mutinied in 1779 when they were ordered to depart to fight the Americans. Refusing to board transport ships, other troops were brought in to force them on board. In the subsequent fighting men on both sides were killed. (Highland regiments, it has to be said, were prone to mutiny frequently in this era.) The established British military reaction to Highland troops can be gauged by the attitude of General James Wolfe, a veteran who had fought the Jacobites while serving under Cumberland in Scotland. He was happy enough to have these intrepid soldiers fight the French in his campaign in Canada as they were eminently expendable. Earlier in his career he had advocated using this 'secret enemy' for the greater military good: if the Highland troops died, no great loss. While in Scotland in 1751 he hatched a bizarre plan to have a suicidal squad of Highlanders under his command assassinate the chief of the Macphersons and then eliminate the whole clan. Luckily, the mission did not proceed. A century later the cult of the Highland soldier was at its Victorian height, and earlier controversial events had been forgotten. Highland, Jacobite and imperial traditions were proudly woven into the identity of various Scottish regiments.

The Scots and Irish had been arriving in America for generations before the final Jacobite war, along with others, and there is an enduring modern belief that a large number of defeated Jacobites from the British Isles were transported as prisoners to the Americas and suffered the fate of being indentured servants there for long periods. As we will see, the numbers were not so great as some modern writers imply. Ian Adams states that 866 captured Jacobites accepted the king's mercy. This meant acknowledging guilt, swearing loyalty to King George II, and agreeing to have their liberty purchased by anyone who chose to purchase them for seven years as a servant in the Americas or West Indies. Apart from those who became indentured servants, smaller numbers were banished to America without this, or exiled in non-British lands.

The distorted perception of mass Jacobite transportation/enslavement perception rests uneasily on the concept that there was an even more long-standing industry shipping white (mainly Irish and Scottish) prisoners and indentured servants. These, say supporters of this idea, were sold into forced labour during the seventeenth and eighteenth centuries in huge numbers. This has unfortunately been seized upon by those who have issues with the concept that the slave trade overwhelmingly victimised people of colour. Apart from certain people with a right-wing slant, the theory has also found popularity with some elements in the Celtic nations as a bolt-on addition to historical grievances, which was purposely hidden for centuries, though it was nothing of the sort. To be fair, those who wrote about this facet of history using the emotive term 'white cargo' may not have intended to sensationalise the issue to the extent that has happened. In reality, there were significant numbers of desperately disadvantaged people who either sought a new life in America and the Caribbean or were coerced into doing so, and who pledged to work as unpaid servants for a period of years after their passage to recompense the costs of the journey.

Numbers of Scottish prisoners and of Jacobites sent to America and the Caribbean islands were not large. One estimate states that there were only 600 Scottish prisoners sent to the West Indies between 1707 and 1763. Following the 1715 Jacobite rising, 1,700 prisoners were held and many hundreds of these were sent on to American colonies, plus around 170 to the Caribbean. Among other vessels, the *Susannah* and the *Wakefield* carried some 185 indentured Jacobite prisoners who were landed in North Carolina.

More Jacobites – 290 in total – were sent west in the summer of 1716 on four ships, the *Friendship*, the *Goodspeed*, the *Elizabeth* and the *Anne*. In the same year, four ships embarked from Liverpool with nearly 160 Jacobites and deposited them on various Caribbean colonies. Conditions on the plantations in the West Indies were generally worse for the prisoners than on mainland America, and a seven-year indenture was sometimes considered little better than a death sentence. Transportation and forced servitude for a set number of years, following a pledge of loyalty to King George, was certainly preferable to facing execution or other severe punishments. Even still, many prisoners refused to sign indentures.

Out of the 126 prisoners on the *Elizabeth* and *Anne*, ninety-seven refused to sign indentures. These ships were under control of captain Edward Trafford and the prisoners had been taken after the Battle of Preston in November 1715. The ships had planned to discharge the human cargo at both Virginia and Jamaica. But the captain was able to sign over all the prisoners to those in Yorktown, Virginia, when he landed there in October 1716. America was crying out for fit, young men, especially those with skills, and the Jacobites also had the advantage of not being common felons who were so often transported across the Atlantic and were doubtless a blight to colonial society. The plantation owners on the islands were also disinclined to accept white indentured servants as they would die more quickly than the African slaves who were better suited to be worked hard in the hot climate of the Caribbean.

There was a natural tendency among some of those in servitude to seek to duck out of their contracted terms, which was usually seven years. On 28 August 1717, Governor Hart of Maryland issued a proclamation ordering local people to be watchful for Jacobite prisoner-servants who sought to escape before the end of their indentures. Meanwhile, it is worth noting that the Scots were not the only ones to suffer for the cause in the aftermath of the 1715 Jacobite rebellion. Many hundreds of men were captured after the Battle of Preston. It was notable that thirty-three men were hanged locally, in north-west England, to teach those rebellious English Jacobites of that region a bloody lesson.

Some transported Jacobites were able to buy their indenture from the captains of the ship and arrived in the colonies as free men. Other indentured men, still able and willing to fight, found themselves engaged in another conflict. The governor of South Carolina himself purchased the indentures of as many of the 185 former Jacobites who came to his territory as he could afford. They were given arms and sent to fight the native Yamasee tribal confederation. Some Jacobite prisoners doubtless found some kind of fellow feeling among communities in places like Carolina and Virginia where there were thriving groups of immigrants and descendants from Scotland who had come there of their own choice. Voluntary emigration to America had previously mainly been a Lowland phenomenon for Scots, but there was increased movement from the Highlands from the 1730s into the nineteenth century. North Carolina had a Scottish governor named Gabriel Johnston, whose presence and policies encouraged a Highland influx that began slowly in the late 1730s (with settlement mainly on the Cape Fear River, later called Cumberland County) and grew notably in the period after the French and Indian War ended in 1763. Johnston (who was governor from 1734 to 1752) was accused of being too lenient with ex-Jacobites. One of these was William McGregor, a convicted Jacobite from 1715, who was made a justice of the peace in 1745.

It's notable that all the transported Jacobite prisoners following 1715 and 1745 were landed in the southern and middle parts of the American colonies; none in the north. Foreshadowing the principles of the American Revolution perhaps, some colonial authorities, while not notably Scottish, still questioned the merit of the whole business. A prisoner who was sent to Maryland on the *Good Speed* (one of fifty-five Jacobite men) named John Chalmers managed to get the local council to debate the legality of transportation.

The labour sentence imposed upon the indentured Jacobite servants in America was hard in most cases and a great number of them did not survive the seven-year period to become free people. Of those who did, most simply vanish from history and we don't know their fate. But there are occasional glimpses of those who survived and prospered. Among the 112 rebel prisoners transported to America on 13 October 1716 was Francis Hume, younger brother of Sir George Hume of Wedderburn. Very fortunately for him, Francis was related to Governor Spottiswood of Virginia, who made him a factor for his estates. His nephew, and another convicted Jacobite, was George Hume, who came to America in 1721 and found employment as a surveyor. He gained large tracts of land, served as a justice of the peace and was commissioned in the colonial militia. Among the wide circle of friends accumulated before his death in 1760 was George Washington.

A famous escape was made by the Jacobite prisoners aboard the *Hockenhill*. This vessel, together with the *Scipio*, the *Two Brothers* and the *Africa*, carried nearly 160 prisoners taken after the Battle of Preston. The thirty prisoners on the *Hockenhill*, abetted by some of the crew, seized the ship, which left Liverpool in June 1716 bound for St Kitts and sailed it back to Bordeaux in France, where they received a warm welcome. They then happily sold off the cargo of the ship and went on their way as free men. The men landed in friendly France still faced the dilemma of what to do in a foreign nation without any means to support themselves. The more upper-class escapees wrote to their friends and the exiled Jacobite court asking for financial assistance. Of the rest, some were tradesmen who were able perhaps to find work where they landed while others may have perilously made their way back to Scotland.

Some prisoners of war after the 1745 rebellion had a similar lucky escape en route to servitude. On 28 June 1747 a British ship named the *Veteran*, which was travelling between Liverpool and the Leeward Islands and carrying 150 prisoners (including some women and children), was attacked and captured near Antigua by a French privateer, the *Diamond*, commanded by Paul Marsat. The freed prisoners were taken to Martinique, a French-controlled island. The British government protested and asked for the return of the Jacobites; the French refused. Some of the Scots enrolled in local French military units (and a few deserted from them), but the fate of the majority is unknown because a volcanic eruption later in the century destroyed official records.

The situation for captured Jacobite fighting men after the '45 uprising was generally more grim. Out of 3,463 prisoners (men, women and children), 936 were shipped to North America and 348 banished. Of those remaining, 88 died of wounds and 120 were executed. At least 425 captives were sent out from Tilbury and Liverpool, the prisoners of war bound for Barbados and Jamaica, to be harshly used as servants on the plantations there. Many mercantile Englishmen saw a lucrative business haggling with the authorities over the cost of each Jacobite dispatched over the sea. London businessman Samuel Smith had connections across the Atlantic and saw a profit to be made on the sale of prisoners at point of arrival. However, he was frustrated by prisoners escaping from English prisons and even ships before the journey began. He proposed the death penalty for those prisoners who managed to come back to Britain and Ireland before the period of their indenture was elapsed. Smith reckoned that he had shipped 453 prisoners from both Liverpool and London by the end of 1747. Liverpool merchant John Hanbury shared in the government contract to transport the rebels. The 1745 rebellion caused a greater threat to the Hanoverian British state than the 1715 uprising had done. The authorities were more scared; a heavier weight of justice had to be dispensed. Despite this, the lives of those Jacobites forced into being servants must have been variable, though even those of them who had to endure hard labour of different types would have had a higher status and better physical conditions than those millions of Africans imported or kept as slaves. Again, because of sympathy from Scottish-descended residents in the south of America or those who were Catholic like some of the transported prisoners, some indentures were bought by colonists and the men immediately given their freedom. Full records of where these Jacobite prisoners landed and what became of them are not known, though most of them were in origin from either the Highlands or the North-East and East Central Lowlands. Maryland seems to have received 155 Jacobites but none at all came ashore in Virginia. The records for the West Indies are more complete, with names, ranks, place of origin often recorded. While the combination of voluntary emigration and prisoner exports (including Scottish Jacobites) hardly made an ethnological dent in the population of what became the United States, it may have been different in some of the West Indies. The *Virginia Gazette* in June 1767 reported that nearly two-thirds of those in Jamaica were Scottish, mostly of course merchants rather than Jacobites of any sort. A few men with Jacobite sympathies had fled to Jamaica after 1746. Most Scots there, as well as Englishmen, would have been involved in plantation estates employing slaves as well as indentured servants. It is interesting that there was a significant presence of Episcopalian Scots in the West Indies even before the union of Scotland and England in 1707, and they were not well-disposed towards the Hanoverians. A Scot named George Duncan, who was arrested in Barbados in 1700 for sedition, had declared, 'the Scotch were as good as the English, no subjects of King William, and that there would soon be a change'. In 1704, Scots on that island refused to accept the proposed non-Stuart succession after the death of Queen Anne.

How many transported Jacobites were able to withstand the period of servitude and foresee the opportunities that the New World perhaps offered them afterwards? Many, likely most, survived their ordeal and a high proportion of them must surely have counted themselves lucky. Those Jacobites at the top end of the social scale had mostly been syphoned off by the English judicial system, denounced as traitors and executed. Even among the rank-and-file prisoners of war, there was a chance that their allegiance might culminate in death. One in twenty prisoners of the '45, in common with those of the earlier rebellion, was chosen by lottery to face trial on the charge of treason and stood a high chance of forfeiting their lives.

A vivid relation of the processing of a captured Jacobite through his voyage to America was given by Alexander Stewart to the Reverend Robert Forbes, who was dispatched on the ship *Gillder* from Liverpool in mid-1747. Attempts were made, pre-journey, to get him to sign a 'charter' agreeing to his indenture, but he stoutly refused to do so. His sea voyage was fairly uneventful, though the vessel was pursued by a privateer just before it made land. Just before he was brought ashore, a senior crew member came to Stewart and made a fine speech about the goodness of the land he and the others were going to. If only they would sign up to seven years' servitude, they would serve a shorter term and then be given 'a gun, a pick and a mattock, and a soot of cloths, and then we was fre to go thorou any place'. Stewart persuaded all the other prisoners to say no to signing the indentures. He was threatened with imprisonment until he signed. Onshore, several 'buckskins' (men born in the Americas) were brought in to bully them into signing. Even though the chief among them, Cornel Lee, was a 'monstrous big fellow', Stewart did not give in. His freedom was bought by a kindly man and he was treated with great civility until, only a few months later, he was able to embark upon a ship that brought him swiftly back to Scotland. His experience was doubtless exceptional, for he informed Forbes that only one other who had been transported with him had managed to similarly get a swift passage home. Several recalcitrant Scots came before the colonial authorities charged with announcing Jacobite sentiments against King George and his crew, but these were few and far between.

The misery of others on that dark adventure on the road to America is made clear in other accounts. An English surgeon named Minshaw was sent to examine the Jacobite prisoners held on the *Pamela* in the Thames in August 1746 and his account (reprinted in Morgan & Rushton, *Banishment in the Early Atlantic World*, p. 96.) is redolent of the disgust he found. Seven vessels had transported around 570 prisoners from Inverness to the Thames in May, Minshaw was tasked with getting details of the men and reporting on their condition on the *Pamela* at Woolwich. Some of the fifty-four men were only able to crawl up the ladder to the deck at a snail's pace; eighteen were utterly unable to climb up. There was a malignant fever below deck and a combination of diseases including an 'odious distemper peculiar to Scotchmen'. He feared that they would all perish, but nothing was done of course. Lice were prevalent in these appalling conditions. One Jacobite prisoner transported south on a ship from Inverness states captives were often dunked in the ocean to rid their bodies of endemic lice; often, the prisoners themselves were drowned. The deaths did not seem always accidental.

By March 1747, prisoners at Tilbury had been held on their prison ship for more than eight months and less than fifty of the original 157 were still alive. The survivors were given food by locals and sympathetic visitors. Many captured Jacobites had earlier been confined in gaols in the north of England. In York, 227 prisoners were held in appalling conditions in February 1746, and it was reported the steam and the stench were appalling. Some Jacobite officers were marched through Southwark and subjected to the malice of the local population before being confined. Some were taken out from gaol to be hanged and their mangled corpses were returned for several days to lodge with their comrades as a further punishment. For survivors in English gaols, shipment to America may have seemed not too terrible.

An intriguing 'what if' of history lies in the fact that it was wondered whether there was a future for Prince Charles Edward Stuart as the ruler of the United States after his attempts at claiming the throne of the United Kingdom so spectacularly failed. The defeated prince may not have taken the suggestion seriously since it appears to have been a measure of how desperate some of his followers were to find a suitable place for him in the post-Culloden world. It was even more unlikely than the idea that he should throw his hat into the ring for the kingship of Poland. At least there, he had a blood tie to the proposed country of rule through his descent on the female side from the Polish royal family. To be fair to him, the prince rejected the idea of an American monarchy immediately it was put to him on the basis that a royal throne there would be incompatible with the cherished aim of becoming king of England and surrounding nations. Suspicions that the ageing Charles Edward Stuart or his supporters were in league with elements of the revolutionary-minded citizens of America may have been largely reflective of the worries of the British establishment, who were keeping a feverish eye on both camps. Italian gossips reported contact in 1775 from some Bostonians inviting Prince Charles Edward to lead them against the British. If this is true, Charles did not take the bait. Three years later another rebel group allegedly invited him over the Atlantic and there is the vague tradition that the French proposed to take him in the vanguard of their army challenging the British in North America. It once more came to nothing. Yet people have occasionally wondered what would have happened had that restless rash adventurer (as someone called him) chanced his fate in the colonial arena.

A surely imaginary account of the Young Pretender's association with America was published by Michael Lafosse in his book *The Forgotten Monarchy of Scotland* (1998) and by others including the conspiracist historian Laurence Gardner. He states that four prominent Americans visited Prince Charles Edward in Rome in 1782. He was assured that the new nation was not entirely given over yet to republican sentiment and a large part of the population were in favour of a more enlightened monarchy than that of the official British state. Charles demurred on the basis of premature old age and lack of an heir, but admitted he would have jumped at the offer ten or fifteen years previously. 'I have failed most of my life,' he stated, 'and have no wish to fail more.' And so, he nobly declined the gift of the New World in the fictitious interview.

Some of those in America with Jacobite sympathies simply got on with their lives in their new country irrespective of the momentous events that the continent went through. Partly as a means of pacifying the Highlands (and to utilise a known resource of fine fighting men), Scottish troops were integrated into the British army and played a part in defending the North American colonies in the French and Indian War (1754–63), which was related to the larger conflict between European powers in the Seven Years' War in the same period. On the other side of the battle lines was a French colonial force that contained admittedly small elements from Ireland and Scotland who had been involved to some extent in the Jacobite struggles in the previous decades.

The Scots, Irish, and Scots-Irish had a poor reputation in late-colonial North America, a country that was still overwhelmingly Anglocentric in ethnicity and outlook. Celts from these nations were sometimes ill-regarded by Anglo-Saxon Americans on account of their origins, their low-class status, poverty and their religion, whether they were Catholics or Presbyterians. Some Irish immigrants with Jacobite associations came to their new American lives via Europe, since a large number of Irish troops went to France in the wake of the Jacobite defeat at the Battle of the Boyne in 1690. One example of this was Owen O'Sullivan, born in France in 1692, son of an exiled Jacobite officer. He went to Ireland and later to New England, where he became a teacher. One of his sons became a major general in the revolutionary army and another was governor of Massachusetts.

America did not look favourably on the Jacobites, who were trying to wrest Great Britain back for the deposed Stuarts: the conflict was sponsored by malcontent Celts in a land far away and even those in America who were perhaps feeling the stirrings of discontent with colonial rule did not link their aspirations for freedom with the Jacobites. Taking advantage of the union of the English and Scottish nations after 1707, plenty of Scots were not inclined to be Jacobites, but saw the new realm of Great Britain as a huge opportunity for advancement. Such 'loyal' Scots were still often looked upon as inferior by English people and by Americans. Americans who wanted to break free from Britain noted a number of adversarial Scots in high places of the colonial government. Large numbers of alien mercenaries – 'dregs of Irish and Scottish desperadoes' – were also seen as a nuisance by Americans. Just before the revolution, there was a steady influx of Highland Scots, including 400 under the leadership of prominent members of Clan MacDonell who settled mainly in the Mohawk valley. One of their leaders was John MacDonell of Scotus, a Scots adventurer educated in Rome, whose military service included fighting for Spain and later for the Jacobite cause in the '45 rebellion. He later emigrated to the province of New York and his people remained as loyalists in the ensuing conflict between British and Americans. He was forced to migrate again to Upper Canada after the Revolutionary War and his family became a prominent figure there, his son Miles becoming first governor of what later became Manitoba. Yet his compatriots, mainly Episcopalian and Catholic Highlanders who had been severely affected by reprisals after Culloden, were reluctant to antagonise British authorities once more. Few in colonial America had the appetite to even mutter vaguely Jacobite sentiments, though the authorities were on the lookout for any sedition. Even in areas like Maryland and Pennsylvania, where there were relatively large numbers of Catholics, there were few accusations of Jacobitism. To colonists on the eve of their own revolution, any British or Irish person who was or had been a Jacobite was an ally of the French and the French themselves who were still actively opposing the British colony. The last phase of the French and Indian War, termed King George's War (1744–48), was still causing disruption. For several reasons, probably including a lack of significant numbers, the French did not think it worthwhile to foment the embers of Jacobite resentment among the British and Irish who had recently settled in America.

Still, there were many individuals whose relationship with the young republic, Jacobite ideals and loyalty to the British establishment was extremely fluid. This was due more to the changing political landscape and changes in their society than to personal beliefs. Some people managed to pledge their loyalty to entirely different ideals at different times in their lifetime without any suggestion that they were disloyal to any earlier service. As an example, we might cite the Scottish medical and military man Hugh Mercer. Born in 1726, he was present on the Jacobite side at the Battle of Culloden and was obliged to go overseas to escape British reprisal. He practised medicine peacefully for the better part of a decade in Pennsylvania and then took up arms in the colonial army, befriending along the way one George Washington, and ably fighting the French. During 1775, when revolution was brewing, Mercer was excluded from the newly raised American regiments in Virginia on account of his being a Scot. However, he overcame this prejudice and found a means to take up arms again, fighting the British authorities. Mercer met his end bravely facing a group of British soldiers in an encounter in January 1777 and ensured himself a place in legend by the bravery of his death. One of his descendants was the renowned General George Patton.

Another combatant at Culloden was Alan Maclean, a native of Mull. He fled after the Jacobite defeat in Scotland and gained a commission in the Scots Brigade in the Netherlands. An amnesty several years later allowed him to return home and he gained a commission in the British army. He served with distinction, if unspectacularly, with British forces, defending Quebec against the American insurgents, and gained his initial commission from fellow Scot, John Campbell, 4th Earl of Loudon. Loudon had been actively involved in fighting the Jacobites as a close confederate of the Duke of Cumberland. Unlike many others in Cumberland's forces, Loudoun did not have a blanket hatred of Highlanders and was prepared to accept that some of them were loyal to the state. He similarly worked with different ethnic and local groupings when he gained high command in North America and was opposing the French. His short command was not considered a success and he was recalled to Britain. A later Scot who had a prominent command was James Murray, son of Lord Elibank. As governor of Quebec from 1760, his background caused him considerable trouble. His brother Alexander was the primary player in the Jacobite Elibank Plot of 1752, and James had to spend most of his career constantly rebutting claims that he had similar anti-Hanoverian sympathies. His time in Canada was also marred by the common North American prejudice that automatically equated Scottishness with Jacobitism, though he was more successful with the pacification of the French-speaking population after British rule was imposed upon them.

Some former Jacobite Scots who were not overtly active in the tumultuous wars in America also sometimes led adventurous lives and achieved notoriety from their shifting loyalties. Their stories display all the elements of complex lives that show that the priorities and political realities of life in America were not a simple case of choosing one conviction and following it through a straight line for the entirety of life. A tale is told about some Highland troops who were captured by the French at the Battle of Carillon in 1758. While they huddled together and awaited an uncertain fate, a French officer nearby roughly shouted at the guards holding the prisoners. Then, to their horror, the man addressed them in their own native language, Gaelic. The Highlanders superstitiously assumed that the French officer must in fact be Satan himself, for no Frenchman was ever known to have spoken their tongue. In fact, the officer was a Scottish Jacobite who had migrated to France after the uprising and then enlisted in the French army. True or not (and it's strangely reminiscent of the Alan Breck Stuart Canadian anecdote), there were numbers of displaced Irish and Scots in the forces facing the British in the New World.

Many inconspicuous Scots from pro-Stuart backgrounds busied themselves with self-advancement in the Americas, usually living in conformity with the establishment. One such individual was John Stuart, who became an Indian agent in Cherokee country. A businessman from Inverness from a notably ardent Jacobite family, Stuart migrated to Charlestown in the late 1740s and became involved in mercantile trade, with varying success. He greatest accomplishment perhaps was forging a lifelong alliance with the Cherokee nation, particularly with the chief Attakullakulla, which led to him being appointed British superintendent of Indian affairs in the south. He held this post until he died in 1779, at which time he owned extensive lands in the region as well as several hundred slaves. Despite his family background, there is no record that Stuart himself actively supported the Jacobites, and his last years were overshadowed by trouble because of his enduring support for the British crown.

Yet some other notable former Jacobites served with distinction for the newborn nation of America during their revolution and deserve honourable mentions. One of these was Angus McDonald (1727–78), the noted Virginia militiaman. Fleeing Scotland after being declared a rebel after serving as a lieutenant at Culloden, he became a merchant in Virginia and was later a captain in the French and Indian War and later came out of military retirement to act as a lieutenant colonel in local revolutionary military forces. He was a member of Clan MacDonell of Glengarry and distantly connected with those MacDonell loyalists noted earlier.

In the end, America was merely a 'might have been nation' for the Jacobites. Had the upheaval of the American Revolution come hard upon the heels of the 1745 Jacobite rebellion and if the leaders of that lamentable enterprise shown more foresight, some may have found a congenial home in America. The generation between 1745 and the establishment of the American republic, as we have observed, saw a seismic change in the world order. We can still wonder what may have happened if various scenarios had played out. Leaving aside the fantasy of Bonnie Prince Charlie becoming king of America (which even he found ridiculous), what would have followed if the Duke of Cumberland had his way and whole clans (specifically the Camerons and Macdonalds) were transported to the West Indies and possibly America to form new colonies? He advocated mass forced emigration because, 'while they [the clans] remain in this island their rebellious and thievish nature is not to be kept under without an army always within reach of them'. Would the displaced clans have acted differently to those cowed, loyal stragglers from the Highlanders who accepted British rule even after the revolution to their own great cost? There were others who had advocated mass clan exportation, though some voiced worries that any displaced clan might transfer allegiance to the French in the New World. We will never know for sure. America remained a minor destination for the flotsam cast adrift by the Young Pretender's failed gamble. Most high-ranking Jacobites integrated themselves more successfully with networks in continental Europe. One faint connection between the Jacobites and the revolutionary Americans is the detectable ideals of freedom spread by the Scottish-rite masonic lodges in the former colony, which allowed men like Washington and many others to formulate their ideas in a conducive environment. But the first ruling Americans were overwhelmingly English in their origins and few indeed among them would have favoured an intellectual lineage from barbarian Scotland.

From the other side, some surviving Jacobites watched the defeat of Great Britain by the American colonists with some irony. Lord Elcho, the disillusioned veteran of Culloden, found himself wondering why London had not permitted individuals like him to return to his homeland after three decades of exile, while at the same time the British grovelled pathetically to their former American colonists. The British treated the Scottish rebels with 'the utmost haughtiness, hardship and cruelty after having vanquished them'. He brooded with bitterness on the difference of treatment. Scots of good birth had laid down their lives for the dubious British cause in America, after all. If some thought the revolution there was a war of liberation, others who were still suffering from the vindictiveness of British justice viewed it merely as a faraway war between two competing sets of Englishmen from the old and new worlds.

Chapter 10

The Last Heirs: Henry and Roehenstart

The contrast between the last royal Stuart siblings, Charles Edward and Henry Stuart, grew starker as their lives progressed. Following his forlorn attempt to claim their father's crown in 1745 and his subsequent inability to gain further meaningful support in Europe, Prince Charles Edward proved increasingly unsuitable as a candidate for that diminishing prize. His younger brother Henry was fundamentally unambitious in supporting his family's royal claims and opted for a more secure role in the Roman Catholic Church soon after the last Jacobite uprising.

Henry still supported the royal dignity (or pretensions) of both his father and his wayward brother while they were alive and always maintained the style of his own high-born heritage until his last impoverished days as a prince of the Church. Yet he recognised himself as rather too passive to be a meaningful player in the martial or mercenary diplomatic power play of the mid-eighteenth century. While Henry was spirited and musical as a child, captivating some observers, he became notably duller as he matured. His reticence led him to a religious life, which suited him well, though his patience was sorely tried at times by his wayward sibling.

Prince Henry Benedict Stuart was born in Rome in 1725, five years after his more famous brother, and was immediately bestowed with the title of the Duke of York. The royal brothers, sons of the Old Pretender, were reasonably close as children, though a true picture of their respective characters is sometimes hard to glean because of the over-reverential praise heaped on them by exiled Jacobite commentators. In their youths, these two exiled siblings in Rome naturally attracted much attention. The elder brother and heir to the Stuart destiny, Prince Charles Edward, was deemed by some to be somewhat frivolous, though he won admirers because of his positivity and personality. Others remarked he was the better looking and had more winning manners. Young Henry had a happy disposition as a child though he became notably more sombre as he grew older and was certainly less inclined to reckless adventure when his youth was some way behind him. One of the most interesting and inaccurate estimations of young Henry comes from Sir John Murray of Broughton, who became Jacobite secretary of state during the 1745 rising. He heaped immoderate praise of both brothers but allowed his imagination to run away with him when he declared that Prince Henry was imbued with the legendary military prowess of his Polish great-grandfather, King John Sobieski, who had heroically defeated the Turks and saved Europe from Islam. The only attributes they had in common was a general good nature.

Henry was more academic than the heir Charles, though that was not a difficult achievement. One criticism levelled at the brothers was they were not educated up to the standard expected for rulers. This sometimes went alongside a slur on their mental abilities. In 1740 the Président de Brosses said of the two royal Stuarts, then aged 20 and 15, that they were of mediocre intelligence and less developed than they should have been. From his father, Henry inherited of course his royalty and an unshakeable loyalty to the Church of Rome, which invalidated his right to rule by the majority of his supposed subjects in the British Isles. He was lucky, in a way, that he was not inclined to favour the more ascetic form of Catholicism favoured by his mother, Queen Clementina, who was wholly wrapped up in prayer and abstinence in her later years. Her unwavering devotion to prayer and good works was so notable that she narrowly avoided becoming a saint. For all his religious devotion, Henry was devoted to good living and luxury throughout his life. In his boyhood, some commentators said that he was the better of the siblings, though observers were often tainted by their own pro- or anti-Stuart prejudices. In his later years, when he was the sole living heir of the dynasty, Henry was regarded rather as a living fossil and a relic of a bygone age, an uncomfortable position he shared to some extent with the long-estranged widow of his brother.

When the Young Pretender precipitously left France, with minimal support, and launched his rebellion by landing in Scotland, the rest of the royal family (as well as other leaders) were left playing catch-up. The boys' father, James Francis Stuart, was stirred out of his usual lethargy but did not take any decisive action that would have supported his adventurous elder son. Henry went to France where, together with various exiled supporters, he tried in vain to get the French government to quickly raise a fleet to invade England. His brother Charles was now unexpectedly in a position of some power in Scotland and the quick opening of a second front against Great Britain in the south might have been decisive in the Stuarts' cause. However, the French procrastinated and it was more due to their lukewarm reaction than to Henry's undoubted inexperience that the hoped-for support fell through.

Henry was treated with contempt by some of the French leaders he needed to win over, not least for his unmanly piety. 'You may perhaps win the kingdom of heaven by your prayers,' the Duc de Richelieu told him once, 'but never the kingdom of Britain.' Prince Henry was obliged to linger uselessly on the coast while the Jacobite rebellion withered away in Britain. The rebel army invaded England, reached Derby, then retreated. Then came Culloden. Henry helped to arrange ships to find and carry his brother away from Scotland after the defeat. When the pair was reunited in France, after an interval of three years, Charles did not recognise Henry at first.

It was during this period, considerably disillusioned by the immorality and duplicity he saw in the upper reaches of French society, that Henry decided on a course he had been quietly considering for some time. Vocation to the priesthood was by no means unheard of among the sons of princes, but for an exiled royal family with only one other son on whom to hang its already fragile hopes, it could be considered dangerous. Charles guessed something was amiss shortly after his return for he complained to their father that Henry was hiding something from him. In April 1747, Henry physically fled from his brother, and it soon emerged that he was planning to become a cardinal. The news came in a letter from his father, with whom the younger brother had been plotting his spiritual departure. James Francis Stuart, devout Catholic that he was, naturally welcomed his second son's decision. He also gave two common-sense reasons to back up his support. The first was that he did not have the right or the power to stop Henry becoming a priest. The second was that, owing to the heavy expense that Charles has encumbered the family with his failed attempt to recapture his throne, Henry becoming a cardinal – a prince of the Church, after all – made very good economic sense.

Prince Charles Edward Stuart naturally saw the move as a betrayal and a premature admission that the Stuart venture for the British crown was lost. Some others also saw Henry's career choice in a less than glowing light. The French foreign minister Marquis d'Argenson coldly characterised the younger Stuart sibling as 'Italian, superstitious, rogue, avaricious, fond of ease, and jealous of the prince'. The breach between the brothers was never fully healed. For all his faults, Henry took a pragmatic decision that made clear that he believed there was no viable future for himself at least in any dynastic restoration. It was a notably clear-sighted decision from someone who remained naïve on other matters, especially his elder brother's deteriorating behaviour. The decision, and family deception, also caused an irreparable seismic rift between the Old and Young Pretenders. The latter never saw his father again. Not only did Charles recognise Henry's sudden vocation as a personal affront, he also knew that many Protestants who had formerly looked favourably on the right of the Stuarts to the throne and who might have reluctantly accepted their private religion, could never accept one of that royal family becoming a Catholic cardinal.

Agents for the British authorities continued to carefully monitor Henry following his elevation to the college of cardinals and fretted over the arcane marks of title and distinction that he was given as both a temporal and spiritual prince. Albeit he was no longer in any way a political threat to the Hanoverian crown, they noted with satisfaction that jealousies and infighting at the papal court had not quite given Henry the highest degree of official recognition as the son of a supposed king. There was slight surprise that he was made a cardinal at the age of 22, but this was also not unheard of. Various honours, including the revenues of churches, were bestowed upon the cardinal duke and he was later made Archbishop of Corinth and then awarded the see of Frascati near Rome, which brought with it a grand palatial residence in Rome. His income was bolstered by the revenues of several abbeys in France, while other income was channelled via religious sources in Spain and even Mexico. During his early adulthood, Henry was also receiving funds from his royal father and was passably wealthy. Much of his income was expended on assisting the poor and community of Frascati, entertaining guests, plus supporting worthy petitioners who came to him for support. For all his love of ceremony and the fruits of wealth, Henry was also highly devotional and favoured the company of artists and other worthies to mere wastrels and sycophants.

Shortly before the death of their father the Old Pretender in 1766, Charles Edward and his brother Henry had reconciled. Henry had generously bequeathed Stuart funds due to him to his increasingly dissipated sibling. Following the death of James Francis Stuart, his elder son took on the title of King Charles III and the two brothers met in person for the first time for eighteen years. The respective change in the brothers and their circumstances must have been remarkable. Charles was no longer the dashing young adventurer who had nearly reclaimed a lost kingdom; he was a bloated itinerant leading a wholly unfocused life. Henry, the overshadowed sibling, had now become a dignified and rich potentate of the Roman Catholic Church, widely respected by those in the Vatican and beyond. Yet, Henry's influence could not help him get the papal court to recognise the right of his brother to the British throne. The pope and his advisers were far too wary of the significant power of Great Britain to risk its own position or the situation of Catholics who were, for the while, tolerated in British-ruled lands. While still receiving papal funds, Charles went into a huff and refused to meet the pontiff, though the cardinal duke eventually prevailed on his dwindling better nature (which was being rapidly dissolved in alcohol) and engineered a meeting in May 1767.

Charles Edward was now styling himself the Count of Albany, an adaptation of an old Scottish title that did not quite amount to an admission that he was not really a king. Cardinal Henry bemoaned his brother's drunkenness to prominent Jacobites. Soon the Count of Albany was married and making his brother's life miserable by his behaviour and pressing forlorn claims of getting papal recognition. When Pope Clement XIV died in 1774, British officials in Rome gleefully spread the rumour that the Pretender was now so deluded that he imagined his brother might be elected the new pope. When the drunken and abusive Charles Edward lost his wife, who ran away to a convent and began an affair with the Italian poet Alfieri, the cardinal duke remained sympathetic towards her.

In 1783, Henry rushed to his brother's bedside in Florence under the impression he was dying. However, Charles recovered and revealed to Henry the full extent of his estranged wife's adultery. Henry arranged for the poet lover to be exiled, but he contrived to remain sympathetic to the disconsolate Louise, the Countess d'Albany. He was, for a long time, sympathetic and actively helpful to his brother's estranged wife. But Louise, who survived Henry and all others in the family, was spiteful about him to the last, a tendency she extended to others. 'He is very whimsical and very dull, for he bores everyone he meets,' she told a friend. 'He belongs to a race of amphibious creatures who are intended to be seen from a distance, but whom an evil chance has brought close to our eyes.'

The good-natured but somewhat gullible cardinal duke had another difficult relationship with his brother's only child, Charlotte Stuart, who was Charles's daughter by his mistreated Scottish mistress Clementina Walkinshaw. Due to the cruelty of the Jacobite hero, mother had fled with her young daughter (who was born in 1753) to a convent in France. Charles re-established contact with Charlotte in 1783 and she came to live with him in Florence soon afterwards. Charlotte was legitimised and ennobled as the Countess of Albany and remained with her father until his death. The countess came with her own agenda and own secrets. She was the secret mistress of Ferdinand Maximilien Mériadec de Rohan, Archbishop of Bordeaux and Cambrai and mother to three children: two daughters, Marie Victoire, Charlotte Maximilienne Amélie, and a son, Charles Edward. These 'heirs' were unknown to their Stuart grandfather and everyone else in the higher reaches of the Jacobite court.

Charlotte began pestering her uncle Henry with letters demanding recognition, which he ignored. Through a combination of brash insistence and an obvious devotion to her increasingly ill father, Henry began to see Charlotte in a more positive light, and as she rose in his affections, so he finally lost patience with the estranged wife of his brother, Louise, who had also been causing trouble for several years. But the young countess did not long survive her father. Prince Charles Edward Stuart died in January 1788 and Charlotte Stuart, Duchess of Albany, died in November the following year.

The cardinal duke now found himself without family and with no real supporters to claim the long-gone throne of Great Britain as King Henry IX. He did not press a claim to this title with the pope, aware that it would not have met with success. In private, and in correspondence he retained the royal title, and even upheld the ancient tradition of touching diseased supplicants who hoped to be cured by the king's touch, following a tradition of British monarchs that had endured for hundreds of years. Henry had a sad downturn in his fortunes in his old age, at the end of the eighteenth century, when the world was changing irrevocably. It is a mark of Henry's obstinate and touching duty to the ageless order of things and the divine right of kings that he sincerely mourned the execution of King Louis XVI of France in 1793. Despite the half-hearted and cynical support the French crown had offered his own house, Henry dutifully performed a solemn requiem mass for his soul. Worse was to come several years later when Napoleon's armies threatened to overrun the Papal States and demanded a huge pay-off. Henry was one of those who willingly surrendered his worldly goods and left himself in virtual poverty. Gone were the family heirlooms, including real treasures bequeathed to him by his Polish Sobieski ancestors.

Despite the bribery, French forces surged into Italy and took control of the pope's territories. Henry was forced to flee with many others, first to Naples and then to Sicily, from where he journeyed to Venice. The unlikely saviours who assisted the cardinal in his dire penury were his hereditary enemies, the Hanoverians. There seems to have been a sense among some of the British establishment, and even in the usurping royal house, that the vastly diminishing threat that the Stuarts would ever come back should allow a more indulgent attitude towards them. There was a curious, touching scene in August 1794, before Henry's downfall, when his carriage became jammed in a narrow street in Frascati alongside another vehicle. The other occupant was Prince Augustus Frederick, Duke of Sussex, sixth son of King George III. What might have been an awkward encounter was forestalled by the English prince, who jumped down from his carriage and had the good grace to address his opposite as 'his royal highness' during a pleasant conversation. Sussex also happily visited Henry several times again in his final years. It was said that the cardinal had earlier encountered Prince William Henry, Duke of Gloucester, nephew of George III. He had been one of those who had knelt before him in Rome and received the king's medicinal touch. But the cardinal did not acknowledge his identity. Gloucester's presence perhaps is a token of a growing English, and even a Hanoverian fascination, with the ousted line of the royal Stuarts.

The plight of the poverty-stricken Stuart priest prince came to the attention of an English official in Italy and an appeal was passed through various intermediaries and reached King George III in London. The Hanoverian king immediately awarded him £500 and an annual pension of £4,000. The cardinal was immensely touched and grateful and gave thanks via another English official in Europe, extolling the generosity of 'his sovereign', an acknowledgment that George III was de facto king of Great Britain. What was not mentioned was that Henry had effectively, and for a long time, been deprived of his rightful inheritance from his grandmother Queen Mary Beatrice, widow of James II. Old George may not have personally known about this fact but his government did.

Henry's final years were spent in relative comfort, back in his old familiar homes. As the century changed, he was still able on occasion to take part in the splendid public events in Rome as befitted a cardinal who was in the highest tier of Catholic hierarchy. His mobility suffered and he walked with the aid of a stick that had the likeness of King Charles I carved as its handle. He now lived more simply and, despite his infirmity, retained his youthful looks and a somewhat juvenile cast of mind. Many were entertained at his table who would have been refused entry to the palaces of other high princes of the Church.

These included the curious as well as the Jacobite-minded from his ancestral homeland. Some British visitors found the cardinal amiable but strangely mannered. English was his third language, behind Italian and French, and he spoke it with difficulty, though he was apt to be offended when his English could not be understood. One visitor was the Scottish antiquary Joseph Forsyth, who put up with Henry's awkward jokes, such as his observation that the Scots were blessed with second sight but not foresight. On hearing that Forsyth's grandfather had died for the Jacobite cause, old Henry's eyes filled with tears and he invited Forsyth to sit next to him. Such emotion at the blood shed by several generations of Scots for the Stuarts was readily shown also by Prince Charles Edward and the Old Pretender too. His English chaplain in his final years remembered Henry speaking wonderfully about England, a nation he had never seen, and being overcome by emotion every time he thought of those Scots who had been martyred for the Stuart cause. The chaplain would tell people, even at this late date, that Henry would be king one day.

Henry Stuart died, lost in senility, in July 1807, a remnant of a long-lost order. Few in Great Britain seriously mourned him. King George IV graciously agreed to fund part of his proposed monument. The royal connection was maintained in 1939 when Queen Elizabeth, the queen mother, had a tomb erected above the remains in Rome of Henry, Charles, and their father. In his own light, however, Henry Benedict Stuart, Cardinal Duke of York, forged a highly successful career within the calling of the Roman Catholic Church. Balancing loyalty to the crumbling shadow empire of royal Stuart aspirations, and supporting his exasperating brother financially and otherwise, he maintained a dignified demeanour on all competing fronts through all his long years.

Despite his reconciliation of sorts with the fact that the Hanoverians were secure on the throne of Great Britain and his ambivalent attitude to being King Henry IX, he made one final gesture to appease his Jacobite birthright. He stated in his will that the rightful heir as king of Great Britain was Charles Emmanuel IV, king of Sardinia. So began the shadowy, theoretical Jacobite succession that has passed down to the present through a line of obscure European nobility, none of whom had the faintest interest in claiming this dubious heritage.

The most mundane of the royal Stuarts never achieved or even aspired to the personal following that many of his family possessed. The direct line of the Stuarts perished with a whiff of sanctified incense if not a whisper. There was only the faintest commemoration of this oddly humble prince in the mystical terms that seemed reserved for more ardent leaders. In a strange poem that seems to have come out of South Wales in 1788, an array of Celtic heroes is called up and likened to the legendary Welsh champion Owen of the Red Hand. Among the champions summoned in verse is the rather inappropriate and meek Italian Stuart cardinal:

> This Owen is Henry the Ninth,
> Who dwells in a foreign land.

His brother Charles would have been proud of such a comparison. Henry would have been perhaps perplexed by it.

Alongside the Jacobite succession, which passed to princely families in Europe after Henry's death, there have been others who have put forward their own contentious claims to be heirs of the royal Stuarts. The first notable figure among these was a man surnamed Roehenstart. He was born with the conspicuous forenames Charles Edward Augustus Maximilian in 1784 and brought up by his grandmother Clementina Walkinshaw in continental Europe. His strange surname was a conflation of the names Rohan and Stuart, which perhaps gave a clue to his identity. Charles himself sometimes eccentrically derived the name from the animals roe and hen. In keeping with his royal grandfather, he used a variety of different names throughout his life. While early family letters simply call him Charles, he later became variously August Maximilian, baron and chevalier Roehenstart, Monsieur de Stuart, Korff-Roehenstart, plus other aliases. The constantly shifting identify points to an inner uncertainty and was also a tactic perhaps to throw imaginary enemies off his scent. When he did flag up his noble ancestry, he was ignored by the Hanoverian elite, and indeed everyone else; there was no chance that anyone was actively out to get him. His life was curiously ineffectual from start to finish.

Much of Roehenstart's true history was unravelled by the American scholar George Sherburn in the mid-twentieth century, but the aura of mystery remains around him. The speaker of several languages, he drifted from country to country, never making a success of any enterprise and often spinning a web of half-truths around himself. He claimed, for instance, that his mother later married a Swedish nobleman, who was actually fictitious. One of his other fantasies was that the mild-mannered Henry, Duke of York, had poisoned his mother Charlotte and stolen her Italian estate. (This lie was picked up by the later pretender John Sobieski Stuart in his book *Tales of the Century*.) He also contrarily claimed that the cardinal had repeatedly asked for him before his death.

His various adventures saw this rootless character variously fight in the Napoleonic wars and travel to America between 1812 and 1814. This seems to be fact, though his claim to have been captured by Turkish pirates in the Gulf of Mexico is suspect. For a while he resided in Italy, and he claimed there that he was descended from the royal Stuart family. He had a fleeting encounter with Bonnie Prince Charlie's widow, Princess Louise, and was roundly rebuffed when he said he was related to her. She took an instant dislike to him – probably because he called her 'step-grandmother' – and Roehenstart also detested her. If she acknowledged that he was the grandson of her late husband's mistress, he would naturally bring unpleasant association with him. After praising her intelligence, he damned her with the observation that 'she is malicious and vindictive to a superlative degree'. Rather fittingly, this strange character ended his days in Scotland, in 1854.

Despite claims to the contrary, there is a strong likelihood that he was who he claimed to be, the grandson of Prince Charles Edward Stuart, the son of Charlotte, Countess of Albany, and the Archbishop of Cambrai, Prince Ferdinand Maximilien Mériadec de Rohan-Guémené. Charlotte expertly concealed the existence of her three children from her father and those around him. For many years Count Roehenstart pursued a military career and became a lieutenant colonel, but after he resigned his commission, he spent the bulk of his time vainly pursuing legacies and savings in various parts of the world that always remained beyond his grasp. His claims to these inheritances may have been real, or at least plausible, but the fortunes had long since dissipated in the arcane webs of the international banking establishment. The wealth of the exiled royal Stuart house, probably never great, was lost in the chaos caused by the French revolution and the Napoleonic wars.

In his early years, Roehenstart studied medicine in Scotland and told a few people there about his claims to be the grandson of the Young

Pretender, though his story did not become widely known. He had taken Gaelic lessons in the country and said he hoped to live quietly in the Highlands, an ambition his restless nature did not let him fulfil. This shiftless urge was something he shared with his grandfather. Not everyone believed in his ancestry; he was unsuccessful when, in 1816, he petitioned the prince regent for a pension. Part of his problem seems to have been his love of romance and tendency to weave himself into tall stories of his own making. By 1853, the second of his wives had died (neither marriage produced any children, though one researcher claimed he had four children by his first wife), and the following year he gravitated back to Scotland. He had some contacts in the upper classes of the country and had just visited the Duke of Atholl at Blair Castle when his carriage overturned travelling south and he died from his injuries. His body was buried at Dunkeld Cathedral, not far from the site of the Battle of Killiecrankie in 1689, where Jacobite Highland forces loyal to the deposed King James VII were defeated by the government. His friends provided a simple monument with the inscription, 'Sacred to the memory of General Charles Edward Stuart Count Roehenstart who died at Dunkeld on the 28th October 1854. *Sic transit gloria mundi.*'

While the claims of Roehenstart have been largely accepted by historians in recent decades, there are dissenters, and this is instructive because the world of the latter-day Jacobites, and in particular the world of late Jacobite pretenders, can be a confusing hall of mirrors. Some have advanced the possibility that Roehenstart's mother was not Charlotte, daughter of Prince Charles Edward, but another unidentified daughter of Clementina Walkinshaw by an unknown father. The Scottish writer Compton Mackenzie favoured this alternative ancestry for the baron. However, the available evidence suggests that Clementina only had one child, Charlotte, Duchess of Albany. According to an alternative ancestry, Roehenstart's father was Dr Ferdinand Smyth-Stuart, also known as Augustus Edward Maximilian de Roehenstart. This individual's father was Joseph Stuart de Roehenstart, whose own father Giacomo was a grandson of King Charles II.

Chapter 11

Deaths and Rebirth

As the nineteenth century dawned, the last vestiges of the royal Stuart line withered away. Old Cardinal Henry Stuart, relatively comfortable in his last years following the upheaval of French invasion, was perturbed to receive an invitation to the coronation of the Emperor Napoleon in 1804. His outrage was not so much around the upheaval that the Corsican's armies had caused to the Papal States and his own wealth and lifestyle a few years previously; he was concerned about the fact that the invitation had addressed him as 'cousin' instead of the customary term 'brother' that was due to him as a royal prince on the same social standing. Henry had given up any hope of claiming the British throne decades ago, but still insisted on the dignity of his royal standing even in his final years of relative poverty.

The Young Pretender's widow Princess Louise of Stolberg-Gedern survived until 1824, living in Florence and occasionally meeting British tourists who were amazed to see this living relic of the Jacobite age, who seemed like the last survivor of an ancient epoch of history. She had survived the death of her estranged husband and her lover, the Italian writer Alfieri, and it may have been that she was unphased when, in 1809, she was summoned to Paris by Napoleon. The French dictator questioned her about whether she had any children with Prince Charles Edward, as he was toying with the idea of seeking out a new Stuart Pretender to displace the Hanoverian dynasty in Britain, a recurrent French idea. Louise advised that she had no issue by her husband. She was kept in Paris for a short time before being allowed to go back to Italy. There was little prospect either to use the cardinal, 'Henry IX', as a weapon against the British establishment. Henry was in his seventies, placidly content in his bishop's palace at Frascati, and had no political following. Jacobitism had dwindled from a political royalist movement to a romantic dream. And old Henry Stuart besides was warming to the Hanoverians in his final years, especially since they helped him out when French forces invaded Italy and destroyed his affluent lifestyle. No surprise perhaps that the cardinal cheered when he heard that the French had been defeated by Great Britain at the Battle of Trafalgar in 1805.

Possibly unknown to Napoleon, there was a genuine Stuart descendant at large in Europe at the time in the shape of Count Roehenstart, the grandson of Prince Charles Edward Stuart, who spent some time in France. If the French leader was aware of him, he was either sceptical of his lineage or thought that he was of limited value in using as a tool against his enemy Great Britain. The tradition that the Sobieski Stuart brothers, who claimed to be grandsons of Bonnie Prince Charlie, were honoured by Napoleon and given commissions in his army is as bogus as the brothers' other pretensions.

Napoleon may have harboured occasional vague sympathies with the romantic ideals of the Jacobite cause, in the same sense that he was interested in the Celtic Revival, which resurrected interest in the remote, non-classical past. He was certainly influenced by the concept of France as the successor state of Celtic Gaul, which he could rebuild into a new empire. More surprising is the claim that Bonaparte was himself the descendant of a Jacobite Scotsman. This bizarre story, recently revived by a researcher named Robert Torrens, says that a hedger named William Bayne from Crieff in Perthshire departed from Scotland after the '45 and was shipwrecked in Corsica, where his family remained and intermarried with locals. By an unlikely strangulation of language, his surname became entangled with his fellow associate survivors as 'Bayne and his party,' which mutated into 'Bonaparte', a surname adopted by his son who became ruler of France. This tall story was first briefly mentioned in a book called *Crieff; Its Traditions and Characters* published in 1881, but the work does not provide any details to substantiate its extraordinary claim.

There are other traditions that Napoleon was descended from the royal Stuart family. One story states that his grandfather was given the coded surname *de buona parte*, 'of good family', because he was the secret son of Prince Giacomo Enrico de Boveria Rohana-Stuardo, an illegitimate son of King Charles II, who was born in Naples in 1647 and died in 1669.

Another theory insists that the emperor's grandmother Maria had an affair with another shadowy pseudo-Stuart, Joseph Stuart de Roehenstart, who lived from 1722 to 1783. They had a child who was Napoleon's father. Fables of course flourished around the upstart emperor, and there were several alternative tall tales about his origins. Another story says that Napoleon was the son of the mysterious Man in the Iron Mask, who was conjectured to be the rightful King Louis XIV who was wrongly imprisoned. Leaving those fables aside, in Britain itself, Jacobitism was reborn, after a fashion, and it sprung from the unlikely interest of the Hanoverian rulers of the nation. Scotland's rehabilitation from a nest of wild Highland rebels to a romantic backbone of the British Empire was not a quick or easy process. After the outlawing of the kilt and the persecution of Gaelic culture, came the Highland Clearances, which were a harsh economic rather than a political process. Lowland Scotland produced an extraordinary upsurge in philosophy and thinking in the eighteenth century with dazzling literary luminaries like David Hume and Adam Smith introducing world-class ideas as part of a Scottish Enlightenment. It was as if the nation, deflated by the Act of Union with England and torn apart by the Jacobite wars, was regenerating itself by looking at its own recent past to reinvent its identity.

The chosen identity that Scotland opted for was a strange conflation of ancient Celtic myth and tartan invention, a heady mix of imagination and pseudo-history that has filtered down to the present day. Traditions of the Jacobites, in the form of mythic Highland warriors, fed into the tail end of this misty imagined past. One of the architects of the rebuilding of the nation's psyche was a writer named James Macpherson, who won international fame by supposedly discovering the Gaelic poems composed by an ancient Scottish bard named Ossian, though in fact Macpherson fabricated a great deal of material and tampered with the texts of other traditional material he included in his published works. His books were popular throughout Europe, though his claims were disputed by many people who suspected his hoax. Significantly, the teenage Napoleon was enervated by reading an Italian translation of Macpherson's works. Tales of the ancient Celtic warrior caste inhabited his imagination to the last;

he even enthused about the work to those who took him to his final exile on the island of St Helena.

The strange mutation in attitudes towards the Jacobites in Great Britain possibly happened soon after the echoes of the Battle of Culloden died away. Many after the event felt some ambivalence towards the lost cause of the Stuarts and this attitude was not confined to those in Scotland. Even in England, where supporters of the cause had singularly failed to follow their convictions, there were sporadic nostalgic demonstrations in favour of the old order. There were reports of Stuart support in Bath in 1749, where locals adopted tartan apparel and the Jacobite white rose and sang rebel songs in favour of Prince Charles Edward Stuart. The authorities wisely did not intervene, seeing nothing seriously political in the frivolity. More violent events happened in Staffordshire and elsewhere a couple of years earlier, when disaffected locals wore plaid and spouted Jacobite rhetoric, though these were small-scale demonstrations against local Whig corruption more than true pro-Stuart protests.

In 1773, Dr Samuel Johnson toured the Highlands and Hebrides in the company of his Scots biographer and friend James Boswell. While Johnson's disdain for the northern nation was well known, and standard issue for educated Englishmen of his day, he had a high regard for some aspects of Jacobitism. It is often claimed that he was an ardent Jacobite, but his support for the cause was rather more nuanced and he hated what he saw as the backward and narrow religion of most Scots and he was vehemently scornful of the supposed Ossian fraud of James Macpherson.

A lifelong Tory, Johnson's early support of the Stuarts was founded on a conservative principle that they were the ancient and established ruling dynasty of Great Britain. He did not, Boswell said, hold that common Jacobite belief in the divine right of kings. Johnson came to believe, grudgingly, that the Hanoverians' succession only became rightful after they had ruled the nation without disturbance for several generations. He also admitted that he doubted whether he would have supported the cause in 1745 if he had been called upon to do so. Yet Johnson was attached to the romantic ideals of the lost Stuart cause and called the Jacobite uprising a noble effort. He may have baulked at being seduced by the rose-tinted element of the Jacobite movement, but he was one of the first major public figures to express admiration for their ideals. He was followed in succeeding generations by men like Robert Burns and Walter Scott who had likewise contrary and complex emotions about the lost cause, and who cherry-picked aspects of it to express their own ideals.

The ever-loyal James Boswell carefully edited his hero's positive thoughts on Jacobitism in his biography, though he wrote about them in his journal while the two men were exploring Scotland. Boswell himself, despite having a sneaking fondness for the Jacobites, was a loyal subject of King George III and tied himself up in knots when he included mention of the exiled royal Stuarts in his writings. Should the leader of the '45 be styled Prince Charles or the Pretender? He shuddered at the latter suggestion as being offensive and toyed with the idea of tortuously referring to him as 'the Grandson of King James the Second'. The conundrum drove him to such distraction that he audaciously took the problem to the king himself. King George III hesitated to answer, then admitted it was no matter to him what his supposed rival was called. Poor Boswell's neurotic Jacobite phobia would not be shared by the following generations, whose fascination with the cause would have astonished all those who had been glad to see the extinction of the royal Stuart family.

Chapter 12

The Hanoverian Jacobites and the Nineteenth Century

The curious adoption of Jacobite tradition by the German family that displaced them took place in the nineteenth century. The fleeting encounters between Cardinal Henry and peripheral members of the house of Hanover were perhaps excusable abroad, but even in Britain some members of the new royalty were overtly aware of their predecessors. The English diarist John Croker reported that, in 1828, Princess Augusta (1768–1840), a daughter of King George III, told a friend that she had felt fraudulent calling herself a princess while any representatives of the deposed Stuart monarchy were still alive. After Henry, Duke of York died in 1807, she reportedly announced that 'I felt myself to be really Princess Augusta'. The Hanoverians, under Queen Victoria and her German spouse Prince Albert, were soon bedecking themselves in tartan, and acting out a lifestyle that integrated much of the culture of Highland Scotland (and, by implication, Jacobitism) into their own dynasty. The shameless enthusiasm of the British royal family for Jacobitism and Highland culture that they had previously endeavoured to eradicate was just one bizarre aspect of their cultural appropriation in the nineteenth century and beyond. Just as Queen Victoria became Empress of India and symbolically absorbed the subcontinent within her own being, so she became the very embodiment of Jacobitism. 'For Stewart blood is in my veins,' she reminded her subjects, 'and I am now their representative and the people are as devoted and loyal to me as they were to that unhappy Race.' The regal condescension about her royal predecessors is palpable. And yet she fully believed in a misty-eyed brand of Jacobite that survived for some people in Scotland. On one of her early visits to the Highlands she insisted on being regaled with the rebel song, 'Oh, Wae's Me for Prince Charlie'.

The royal fascination with Scotland, the Highlands and the ghost of Jacobitism began with Victoria's uncle, King George IV. To quell the dissent still evident not far below the surface in the neighbouring nations of England, the king was persuaded to go on two highly daring adventures into what had been enemy territory until very recently. George IV became the first ever British king to set on foot on Irish soil without an attendant army. And, if his arrival evoked distant memories of the last royal visitants, the rivals William III and James II in 1690, the progress was carefully stage managed to avoid controversy. When King George arrived in early September 1821, he was received with a rapturous welcome by a segment of the population in Dublin, Kildare and Meath. Those Irish who were not simply showing signs of loyal devotion to the British monarch (and there were some) were hoping for political concessions for Ireland and for royal support that would bolster their aspirations for Catholic emancipation. In terms of public relations, the visit was a huge success for the king. Never popular in England, George basked in the adoration of a seemingly servile populace and his confidence as a monarch was hugely bolstered. The apparent joy of the crowd greeting him on his arrival was so immense that he announced it was the one of the happiest days of his life. He had long wanted to visit the Irish, he announced, and added, 'My heart has always been Irish…this day has shown me that I am beloved by my Irish subjects…and I love Ireland'. While he may have long wished to visit Ireland, the depth of his commitment to his Irish subjects was open to question. Queen Victoria unwillingly alighted in Ireland in 1849, heavily aware that a burden of duty forced her to be there. The country was still reeling from the potato famine, but this escaped royal attention. The queen noted that she was not enduring a journey of pleasure and soon departed from the benighted nation. In contrast, it is reckoned that Victoria notched up eighty months living in Scotland, while she only visited Ireland for a total of five weeks.

Not to be outdone by George IV's Irish jaunt, prominent people in Scotland began to orchestrate an even more spectacular royal visit to their nation, which eventually transpired in 1822. Scotland too had been much neglected by the monarchy – the last reigning king to venture there was Charles II in 1650. Although that voyage was politically expedient, cementing the support of his ancestral realm in the face of republican opposition, Charles was carefully controlled by Calvinist factions and had a low opinion of the entire nation. The arrival of the Stuart exiles James Francis in 1715 and Charles Edward in 1745 had mixed results of course. In contrast to the Irish journey, George IV's stay in Scotland did not see him far venture outside the vicinity of the capital city. When the king came to Scotland, the nation came to him. What transpired was a semi-comic extravaganza that saw Edinburgh transformed into a citadel bedecked in tartan of all hues, all of them garish and most of them bogus. The itinerary for the king's visit was carefully managed by Walter Scott and aroused both a competing clamour among Scotland's upper classes to take part in the event, plus a widespread amazement in some others about how the city had somehow been transformed into a kilted wonderland. Many objected to the fact that the whole of Scotland had now been Highlandised. Highland landowners and clan chiefs hurried to weavers and ordered what they were told were traditional tartans for their septs, and they were encouraged to bring bands of retainers to the city to represent their clans. Even Lowland lairds who had no affiliations with the garb were suddenly swathed in plaid.

Since the defeat of the Jacobites, Scotland had been seen by some further south as an irredeemable nest of barbarous traitors. The country had only been partially redeemed by the recruitment of large numbers of Highland soldiers into newly formed regiments that saw action on the frontiers of Britain's expanding empire and against enemies in Europe. Scotland bought back its reputation for loyalty, in the eyes of the English establishment, through the expenditure of manpower and in spilled blood.

While the Highlands had suffered a loss of young men to the British army, it was also soon denuded of its general population by landlords of large estates who might either be described as economically realistic or rapacious. Landowners and clan chieftains, or those who came in from outside and succeeded them, started to see tenants in economic terms rather than as members of the same clan. Culloden had been the death knell of the old way of life. It was realised that healthy profits could be made by clearing settlements and either forcing tenants abroad, or else forcing them into small, unfertile crofting plots on the coast and forcing them to be fishermen, an alien way of life to tenant farmers. Many of the sons in the region were away fighting so could not help resist the enforced change. And many places were nearly denuded of young and working-aged men. Communities affected include Gairloch, Wester Ross in 1799, and the Perthshire–Argyllshire estates of Breadalbane, in the same decade, where three out of five farm tenancies had men who had been recruited. The most notorious and largest-scale clearances happened in the far north, in lands owned by the Countess of Sutherland and her husband Lord Stafford. Here, between 1807 and 1821, thousands were displaced from fertile farms. Some houses were burnt; some died; violence and intimidation were used. According to the historian of the clearances, Thomas Devine, 'In its scale and ambition the Sutherland strategy was the most extraordinary example of social engineering in nineteenth-century Britain.' The clearances sporadically continued for several more decades. This was the unseen back story behind the gaudy curtain of the king's jolly jaunt to Edinburgh in summer 1822.

Walter Scott had the unenviable task of choreographing the unwieldy king and managing the events, as well as dealing with the competing demands and complaints of the upper crust of society who were clamouring for attendance in the events that George IV was due to preside at during his short stay. To give him his due, Scott managed his task with equanimity and likely realised that he could not possibly please all those unhappy with the royal visit. It could be said that he was principally responsible for the farce of turning the city of Edinburgh into a laughable carnival of tartan. Scott himself had a profound knowledge of Scottish history and was well aware of the apparent unseemliness of the transformation. But, he judged, it was a price worth paying to keep the king and most other people contented. He was giving most of the people what he thought they wanted, not least the king. And, like those in a similar position in Ireland during the previous year, he believed that the greater good of the nation was being served by this grotesque carnival. To the envy of some, the king invited Walter Scott alone on board his yacht at Leith when it docked there on 15 August 1822.

If the monarch had the decency to retain his royal English attire while in Ireland (and who knows what he would have worn otherwise), he showed no such restraint in Scotland. To the delight of some caricaturists and the genuine horror of many Scots, George went into Caledonian overload when he held a grand levee at Holyroodhouse on the Saturday after his arrival. The royal presence was displayed at one end of the room dressed, significantly, in Stewart tartan. His legs, beneath the kilt, were covered in flesh-coloured stockings. He wore diced hose and a minor galaxy of shimmering brooches, as well as a plumed bonnet that symbolically crowned him, in Highland barbarian style, as the chief of all chieftains. Entering the hall, several guests were genuinely horrified. James Stewart of Dunearn was one of many who had a diminished regard for royalty when faced with the reality up close:

> The king did not seem to move a muscle and we all asked ourselves when we came away, what had made us take so much trouble. He was dressed in tartan. Sir Walter had ridiculously made us appear a nation of Highlanders, and the bagpipe and the tartan was the order of the day.

And yet the damage – or the glorious transformation – was done in a few short days. Scotland was born again as an entirely Highland, tartan, romantic barbarian, noble nation. But reborn as a nation that was safely neutered from its wild, Celtic-Jacobite dangerous past. The bizarre warp in history during those days in Scotland is evidenced by the enthusiastic quote of the *Edinburgh Observer*, a newspaper that thoroughly approved of the visit and what it signified: 'We are now all Jacobites, thorough-bred Jacobites, in acknowledging George IV. This seems to be one of the feelings that stimulate the people here, at the present time, to make such exertions.'

What about the king's attitude to Scotland? It is safe to say that, if he loved Ireland, he also gave his heart to Scotland. If his father had been tolerant to the last faded remnants of the Jacobite movement, George IV was a true romantic convert. He had a collection of souvenirs associated with the movement. During his time in Scotland he coveted, but didn't acquire, a dirk work by Bonnie Prince Charlie during the '45. He had a fascination with the Stuart dynasty and was intrigued by the dramatic life of Mary, Queen of Scots. King Charles I was another Stuart monarch who enervated George's imagination. But his interest also had a less self-indulgent aspect. He engineered the acquisition of the Stuart Papers, a valuable collection of documents associated with the exiled royal family that had been languishing in obscurity on the continent since the death of Henry, Cardinal Duke of York, in 1809. In 1819, he generously donated a sum for the completion of a monument erected in St Peter's Basilica in Rome in memory of King James II, his son and grandsons. James II's remains had been treated with some veneration by Catholics after his death at Saint Germain-en-Laye in France in 1701. Candles were kept burning around his coffin until the time of the French Revolution. One tale says that his remains were desecrated at the time of that upheaval. A contrary tradition says that, when revolutionaries broke into the church, they were amazed by the state of preservation of the monarch's remains. The body was put on public display and there were rumours of miracles around it. King George IV, for the sake of decency and to rid himself of the reminder of a holy, post-mortem rival, ordered the body to be buried in the church in 1824.

The architect of the dazzling charade of the king's visit, Walter Scott, has long since been removed from his pedestal on the summit of Scottish culture. Few now read his books with any enthusiasm outside of compulsory educational settings. People in far-flung places no longer devour his literary outpourings and base operas upon his poems and novels as they once did. Scott links the cause of Jacobitism with Scottish nationalism in novels like *Waverley* (1814) and he cleverly equates the appeal of the Stuart cause with an emotional impulse in his characters, something that chimed with his readers, especially as he shows some empathy for the doomed Jacobite venture. In the end, most of his characters with Jacobite leanings learn the error of their ways and reconcile themselves to the sensible, modern, rational appeal of the Union with England. Yet Scott lit the touchpaper of some sort of Scottish renaissance, even if it was built on strange foundations. For all his loyal British agenda, he remained proudly a Scot, and he drew on a deep well of study that went beyond a trivial antiquarian level about his country's culture and history. Even more neglected than Scott is his contemporary and friend James

Hogg, whose ideas on the past threw up an interesting contrast to the more famous writer's work. In his work *The Three Perils of Woman* (1823), Hogg speculates that the fall of the house of Stuart and the doom of the Jacobites was predestined. The harsh punishments that were carried out in Scotland under Stuart rule in the seventeenth century against the righteous religious movement of the Covenanters guaranteed their fall. Whether this curse on the Stuarts, which the persecuted Covenanters pronounced during the killing times in the 1680s, was founded in a genuine folk belief is debatable, but Hogg makes it an interesting suggestion. Hogg also commented on the depredations of Cumberland and the British army in the Highlands in the aftermath of Culloden. Another of his works was a collection of verse and songs, *Jacobite Relics*, published in 1821, which contains a fair share of verse adding saccharine to the burgeoning myth of Bonnie Prince Charlie.

One of the very minor participants in the tartan pageant in Edinburgh passed unnoticed by the commentators who watched the grotesque events was an extraordinary aged man who was presented to the monarch, the last known survivor of the Battle of Culloden, seventy-seven years before. Peter Grant is thought to have been born in 1714 and took his designation of Auld Dubrach from the farm in Aberdeenshire that his family tenanted. Dubrach was reputed to be the highest farm in Scotland. He pursued the trade as a weaver and tailor, but in the rebellion year of 1745 Grant gave up his trade and enlisted in the Monaltrie's Jacobite regiment. He was pitched into the tumult of the campaign immediately and was commended for his bravery at the Battle of Prestonpans, for which he was promoted to sergeant major in the Jacobite army. Grant was captured after Culloden and taken to Carlisle Castle. But he somehow managed to liberate himself and made his way back, at great peril, to his native Deeside in Scotland. He evaded the British forces looking for him and escaped detection, settling back down into civilian life. He married Mary Cumming, who was more than thirty years his junior, in Braemar and the couple had three sons and three daughters. Mary predeceased her husband, dying at Westside in Angus in 1811, aged 65.

Auld Dubrach lived uneventfully and his story was unknown until he was encountered by chance by two young gentlemen named Smart in the hills of northern Angus. Grant's son had taken a farm in Glen Lethnot and the local men discovered with astonishment that the old man was a living relic of the Jacobite wars. The pair listened to the veteran's stories (he even showed them how to use a broadsword) and decided to raise a petition to the king to support him. According to one story, Grant was presented to King George IV in Edinburgh and the monarch addressed the ancient soldier, 'Ah, Grant, you are my oldest friend,' to which Dubrach answered, 'Na, na, your majesty, I'm your auldest *enemy*.' When asked if he was still loyal to the Stuart cause, he boldly admitted, 'Yes, sir, and I would be ready to give my support again, if needs be.' He was awarded a pension of 52 guineas a year and died at Auchendryne on 11 February 1824. Over 300 people attended his funeral at Invercauld and three pipers played the old rebel tune 'Wha Wadna Fight for Charlie'. Memorials to him were erected locally in Invercauld and at Lethot in Angus. *The Scots Magazine* lauded the old hero shortly after his demise:

> The old man's mental faculties continued unimpaired to the very last; and, possessing as he did, a comparatively good state of health, a retentive memory, a winning and cheerful disposition, a distinct recollection of long past events, many of them nearly a century old, and a certain vivacity and fire peculiar to himself in relating them, it is not surprising that the society of this Highland Patriarch was generally considered very agreeable. As may be supposed, he all his lifetime enjoyed an un-commonly strong constitution, scarcely every complaining of illness of any description, until within a few hours of his death – even then, he seemed almost exempted from bodily suffering; and nature completely wore out, he at last expired without the least murmur of struggle.

Auld Dubrach's remarkable story was repeated in countless books in the decades after his death. But was the legend so clear cut? William Maule, later Lord Panmure, had been approached by the two men who encountered Peter Grant in the Angus hills and it was his initiative to raise the petition to the king. Maule appears in the official records of the state visit to Edinburgh, but there is no mention whatever of the outlandishly ancient Jacobite warrior. If the standard account of the meeting between Hanoverian prince and last Jacobite is colourful enough, a variant adds even more to the event. According to this version (reported decades later in *Caledonia* magazine) the king asked Grant, 'Are you sorry now that you were so very foolish and disloyal in your young days as to enter the service of the Pretender?' The veteran's eyes flashed and his chest heaved with emotion. 'Be ma faith, sir,' he exclaimed, 'I wad fecht for him yet: and yell ne'er be a man like [or you'll never look like] Bonnie Prince Charlie.' The account given in *Records of Argyll* states that King George muttered, 'Take away this madman out of my sight. He ought to be shot; but you can mark him down for £50 a year.' Such an encounter seems too good to be true.

Several accounts of Dubrach insist that he wore the tartan outfit he had donned at Culloden, although some descriptions of it make it appear to be rather more modern garb. The claim that Grant escaped from Carlisle has also raised some suspicions. Official lists show that a mere thirteen prisoners escaped from incarceration in English prisons. Two men known to have escaped from Carlisle Castle were William Sharpe and Robert Wright, in August 1747. Five men attempted to escape in November 1748. A Major Macdonald bribed a guard in the prison, but was found out. The records omit any mention of a Peter Grant absconding.

Dubrach's claim to great age is also dubious. Grant's portrait by Sidney Colvin, now in the Scottish National Portrait Gallery, shows an old man to be sure, but probably not someone over 100 years old. Dubrach was also surprisingly well travelled in his final years, not only allegedly travelling to Edinburgh but also more definitely visiting his gardener son at Dunan in Argyll in 1822, a journey that would have severely taxed a man of his allegedly advanced age. There the sprightly centenarian occupied himself by singing rebel songs and energetically cursing the local Campbell population, and his animated presence was remembered by many local people. Peter Grant appears something of a fantasist, happy for attention in his final years. But perhaps we should allow him some leeway. Dubrach was merely making sure he was personalising (and profiting from) the burgeoning legend of the Jacobites that was coming to life in his later years. Generous minds may merely faintly damn some of his fables with that old Scottish legal verdict of 'not proven'. Those looking to venerate ancient Jacobite heroes might best turn to Gordon of Glenbucket, the man who gave Hanoverian kings nightmares.

Queen Victoria herself came to love Scotland after visiting in 1842, and her passion for the Highlands was shared with her husband Prince Albert. Her mania for Scotland was so overwhelming that she informed the royal governess, Lady Lyttleton, 'Scotch air, Scotch people, Scotch hills, Scotch rivers, Scotch woods are all preferable to those of any other nation in the world.' The honest simplicity of the natives appealed to something equally simplistic in her own nature, and the secluded nature of life in the mountains was a huge contrast to the constricted and stuffy life she had to endure in the south. She and her husband could wander for hours in the hills, unbothered by attention or royal duties, and she popularised the lifestyle in the Highlands in her published journals. She also purchased the estate of Balmoral in 1852 and transformed the glen into royal Deeside. A rebuilt castle for the royal family soon rose among the pines and it was resplendently packed with tartan from foundations to rafters. The linoleum and the carpets were tartan; fittings of poplin and silk were woven into the Stuart tartan.

Her strange attitude to the barely vanquished ghosts of the rival Stuart royal family sometimes pops up in her own writings. In her *More Leaves from the Journal of Our Life in the Highlands* (1884), Victoria records her feelings on encountering the monument to Bonnie Prince Charlie at Glenfinnan. It was one of many historic sites that she made a point of visiting. She described the monument as 'very ugly' and gave a short account of the adventures of 'poor Prince Charles' in the area in 1745 and 1746. Following that she offered her bland summation of her own royal relationship to that elusive shadow in the heather: 'And here was I, the descendant of the Stuarts and of the very king whom Prince Charles sought to overthrow, sitting and walking about quite privately and peaceably.' The darker aspects of the aftermath of the '45 insurrection are not summoned up from the landscape. Adept as she was at integrating contrary cultural identities within her royal personage, some things from the past were still banished to the shadows. And the shadow of the dispossessed dynasty remained a presence, albeit a minor one, in the background of the Hanoverians and Saxe-Coburg-Gothas. There is a rumour that fingerbowls were not placed upon the royal table until the accession of King Edward VII, Victoria's son and successor. The reason was that, in former times, Jacobite sympathisers would pass their hands over the vessel, symbolising their allegiance to the true ruler, the 'king over the water'.

As we have seen, some of the Hanoverians – in private at least – uneasily occupied the royal space that had been vacated by the Stuarts. But they soon became assured that they were rightfully occupying a God-given position. Queen Victoria of course blithely imagined herself as the heiress and embodiment of the former reigning house. Her acknowledgment of the allure of Jacobitism percolated down her family tree, and as her descendants chose to change themselves from the Saxe-Coburg-Gothas into the more brand-conscious house of Windsor in the twentieth century, the ironies of the association between displaced and de facto dynasties became softened by the passage of years. In an echo of the actions of King George IV, just before the Second World War, Queen Elizabeth, consort of King George VI, arranged through the offices of Sir D'Arcy Osborne, British minister to the Holy See, to have a new tomb erected over the remains of the last three male Stuart royals in their resting place in Rome.

Chapter 13
Golden Afterglow

Walter Scott could hardly be blamed for single-handedly resurrecting interest in the Jacobites in nineteenth-century Scotland. The Jacobite era was just one subject that he tackled in his wide-ranging and influential treatment of Scottish history in fiction. There was a fierce appetite in Scotland for tales and traditions of the recent past, perhaps allied to the quickening pace of the industrial revolution, which saw rapid urbanisation and changes in society. The Jacobites crept back into the Scottish consciousness like a disreputable ghost, though there was little initial interest in them elsewhere at the time.

Equally as effective in capturing the imagination of the nation were writers like Carolina Oliphant, Lady Nairne, who wrote effective and well-crafted sentimental songs associated with the lost cause of Jacobitism. Songs like 'Will Ye No Come Back Again?' completed the transformation of the long-gone failure Charles Edward Stuart into the immortal Bonnie Prince Charlie, the dashing hero. Part of the success came not only because of her individual craft; it was because Lady Nairne came from a family that was hardwired into the Jacobite cause and had suffered as a consequence. The lingering sentiment behind the songs was real. There was an enduring demand for this new legend and it sustained itself for many decades, flourishing because it fulfilled a need of people to rewrite their past. For the powers that be, it was also welcome, because it seemed to completely depoliticise the Jacobite cause and turn it into a cosy romantic cult. As we will see, this was not altogether true, but in the early and mid-nineteenth century it seemed to be so. One feature of early collections of Jacobite songs, like the *Jacobite Minstrelsy* (1829), was the emphasis that the subject of the ballads was romantic, chivalrous and noble, but that the actual political cause was wrong, even though the gallant Highlanders had been led into it following the charismatic Bonnie

Prince out of misplaced loyalty. Some press reports on the centenary of Battle of Culloden, when there was an event on the site, voiced the same sentiments.

Painters took up the subject of the '45 and the Jacobites enthusiastically in Scotland, focusing mainly on the noble defeated element of the cause. William Stuart Watson's *The Wounded Jacobite* and Horatio McCulloch's *After Culloden* depicted distraught scenes that played to the sentiments of the viewers. Although some English art followers praised the subjects and the artistry, it can be said that they struggled to tally the art with the embers of significance that the last Jacobite rebellion still had. In 1845, the *Art Union* magazine carried an advertisement praising Thomas Duncan's painting, *Prince Charles Edward and the Highlanders Entering Edinburgh After the Battle of Prestonpans*. The anonymous author was at pains to convey its historical significance for the presumably ignorant English audience:

> We know the Scottish people are divided upon the issue [of the Jacobites]. A century, however, has rubbed down all asperities. Scotchmen will no longer make the question 'Prince or Pretender' cause of mortal quarrel; and even the Sovereign of the House of Hanover (whom God may preserve) will drink to the memory of an unfortunate and unhappy scion of a race of sovereigns long since at rest.

The ultimate sign of establishment approval occurred in 1916 when King George V purchased George Pettie's painting entitled *Bonnie Prince Charlie Entering the Ballroom at Holyrood*, which had been painted in 1892.

More public display also helped the nation heal from its Jacobite wounds. Spurred on perhaps by the upsurge in Jacobite song and literature, there were shoots of interest in Scotland's ancient past emerging from the haze of North Britain (as some unionists liked to term the nation). An impressive monument was erected at Glenfinnan by Alexander Macdonald in 1815 to mark the spot where Prince Charles Edward landed in mainland Scotland. Small societies also dared to link themselves with the Stuart past. In 1839 the Royal Order of Heredom at Kilwinning was reborn. This had been an eighteenth-century Jacobite masonic order, which had close links with Swedish and French masons. The revived society quickly re-established links with Swedish masons. Elsewhere, several Cycle Clubs continued convivially as successors of old-time Stuart societies but denuded of political or royalist involvement. The club run by the Williams-Wynn family in North Wales lasted into the 1860s. The scale of interest in the Jacobites remained at a curiosity level, and no threat to the establishment. Benjamin Disraeli humorously mentioned the alternative, Jacobite succession, represented in his day by the Duke of Modena, in his writings.

The interest in Jacobitism that emerged at the end of the nineteenth century was one element of the questing late Victorian psyche. It was as if, after launching the industrial revolution and exploring and conquering the world, the most adventurous minds in Great Britain turned to an even greater challenge allying the mind and the spirit. And those questing minds often looked to the past for a means to explain their own world and navigate into the future. Medievalism, the occult, Anglo- and neo-Catholicism and the Jacobites were all movements that found the attention of enquiring minds and became features of the thinking or artists and others, particularly in the decadent last decade of the century. Having said that, the Jacobite revival represented the most powerful effusion of pro-Stuart sentiment seen for nearly a century and a half and was more than just a constituent part of a general artistic yearning for times past. Artistic and political endeavours affiliated to the Jacobite past emerged in this period.

One spur for the upsurge of Jacobite sentiment was an exhibition at the New Gallery in London in 1889 called 'The Royal Stuarts'. Its president was the Earl of Ashburnham, who had a deeper interest in the cause of many displaced royal families. Soon there were publications that lauded the cause, such as weekly pro-Jacobite papers named *The Whirlwind* and *The Royalist*, which was in print from 1890 to 1903. A journal called *The Jacobite* caused controversy in parliament in February 1893 when an MP for Belfast chose to stir up dark shadows by asking the Home Secretary whether he could suppress this treasonable publication. The minister, Herbert Asquith, suavely replied that he did not propose to 'give fictitious importance to a foolish and ephemeral craze'. The Ulster MP darkly averred that the Loyalists in his province would rise up unless the magazine was abolished. He would doubtless have heard with horror that three candidates actually considered standing for parliament two years earlier, including Gilbert Baird Fraser and W. Clifford Mellor in North Huntingdonshire. Meanwhile, it was rumoured that some staunch constituents in deepest England were quizzing their sitting MPs about supposed secret Jacobite sympathies.

Aside from this minor controversy, several Jacobite organisations were founded during this time. One was the Order of the White Rose, founded in 1886, which was a small group, albeit with prominent supporters and several overseas branches. It was a conscious continuation of those convivial societies that mixed Jacobite allegiance with social gatherings. Among its rules was an instruction for members to 'keep in mind that the White Rose is the token, not only of Honour to the Royal House of Stuart, but of all Faithfulness of Heart...' Such misty sentiment appealed to many of a more romantic slant. Some contemporaries were unimpressed. A Mr Waters wrote a dismissive article that stated the order's membership was mainly bookworms 'recruited mainly from suburban drawing-rooms. They have formed a sleepy society... read dreary papers on unimportant details of history, and indulge in harmless ceremonies with parchments and rose-water; but they steadily set their faces against all active work.' Other press attention, in so far as it existed, was equally condescending. The conservative *Aberdeen Weekly Journal* called the neo-Jacobites 'a body of harmless but foolish triflers' and insisted that the royal Stuarts 'by their own persistent folly [had] forfeited their kingly inheritance'. The whole business of celebrating Scottish nationality at the expense of the British status quo was an irritant to those who touted the establishment position, and the touchstones of the past were dragged into the light as things to be fought over again by either side. Noting the celebration of the totemic Battle of Bannockburn, where the Scots had defeated the English, an editorial in the *Glasgow Herald* on 17 June 1898 weighed in with a condemnation of dangerous nationalistic sentiment:

> Thanks to the persistence of a few, there has of late years arisen a movement for the propagation of a sentiment which threatens to disgust educated and sensible people with Scottish patriotism altogether ... But why will the professional patriots persist in involving the celebration of the great names of Scottish history in ridicule, and at the same time identifying the patriotism that feeds upon that history with one of the most ridiculous political movements in the history of the whole world?

The proliferation of the new Jacobite groups reflected an uncertainty around the whole Jacobite movement, both in the eighteenth and nineteenth centuries.

What did it mean to be a Victorian Jacobite and how did it differ from being an original one? Those who found a newly kindled love for the Stuarts were not solely attracted by the unfortunately dispossessed remnants of the royal family after 1688. They also wept over the fate of martyred King Charles I and celebrated King Charles II over Cromwell and his republican rabble. Few among them seem to have loved King James VI or I, however.

Another more politicised Jacobite group soon arose. The Legitimist League, founded 1891, had the serious aim of offering the British throne to the representative of the Jacobite line of succession, Maria Theresa of Austria Este. Its ambition was to send elected members of parliament, which it never got close to achieving, and it also politely voiced an aim to 'enlist the sympathies of the People in behalf of the eldest branch of the Royal Family', by which it coyly meant the descendants of the Stuarts. Maria Theresa was the unwitting heroine of an 1896 fantasy publication (*The Jacobite Doctors*) that saw Queen Victoria die and the rightful Stuart descendant 'Maria IV' crowned as British Empress.

One of the leading lights who emerged in the neo-Jacobite movement was Theodore Napier. He was an Australian of Scottish lineage and was one of the first of a notable breed of foreign-born Scots and pseudo-Scots whose distance from the ancestral homeland evoked profound sentiment. (Others in this group included poet Sidney Goodsir Smith and the English-born SNP politician Wendy Wood.) Napier came to Scotland as an energised firebrand and adopted full Highland kit as a political statement, reclaiming it from kitsch nostalgists, and he proudly wore the garb in his native Australia. On his travels, he was barred from wearing the kilt in Hawaii, though he successfully objected and was allowed to go ashore on the islands. That aside, he was one of the first to fuse a clamour for Scottish nationalism with the Jacobite cause, which intensified when he came to Scotland in 1893. Like many involved in similar fringe political and fringe cultures and politics, Napier had a private income that allowed him to indulge his cultural passion. He founded a society in Edinburgh named the Royal Oak Club and published *The Fiery Cross* journal in the first decade of the twentieth century. To some, he was a figure of some ridicule but the emotions he represented and stirred up were real and he faced opposition with admirable steadfastness. Nor were all his notions romantic or backward looking. Some imperialists may have winced at his outspoken comparison of the Empire's harsh treatment of the Boers with the Scottish Highlanders not so very long before.

As well as helping to restore awareness of the Scottish patriot William Wallace, one of Napier's other enduring legacies was the continuing commemoration of the Battle of Culloden at public displays on the battlefield, something which occurs to the present. Napier was an inveterate layer of wreaths at significant sites in Scottish history. His nascent Scottish nationalism, an aspiration for Home Rule, did not aim at breaking up the United Kingdom, even if he railed against the Act of Union in 1707. Despite his and others' agitation for some measure of devolution, the Westminster power bloc adamantly refused to consider it and the momentum for an effective nationalist political machine did not become viable for several decades. It was understandable that these early nationalist groups framed their ideals within romantic, semi-Jacobite contexts to express themselves. Foremost among the movements active in this area, which were not overtly active, was the National Association for the Vindication of Scottish Rights, a notably short-lived pressure group founded by Tories in 1853. Napier was exhausted by his struggle in Scotland and went back to Australia in 1912, where he died twelve years later.

Various people involved in the Home Rule movement had Liberal leanings, while the principles of divine monarchism appealed to a certain high Tory mindset. One notable example of the latter was the English-born Ruaraidh Erskine, who became a fierce advocate for Scottish Gaelic and a founder of the Legitimist Jacobite League of Great Britain and Ireland. The latter organisation was founded by disgruntled members of the Order of the White Rose. One representative of the Legitimist League criticised the White Rose group as being 'Jacobite only in name; its sole business is of an antiquarian kind, and at its few public appearances its members only chatter Jacobite folklore over their tea-cups, or read dreary papers to each other under the exhilarating influence of watery claret'. The fractious nature of the neo-Jacobite groups hardly helped their aims. Nor was their unanimity in their place on the political spectrum.

While Erskine stood unsuccessfully as a 'Scottish Tory Home Ruler' candidate in 1891, he later drifted into more radical political waters on the left. A few of the notable neo-Jacobites likewise had trouble deciding which side they were on politically over the course of their careers, surely a sign of deeper uncertainties in their characters. One example is the English Herbert Vivian, journalist and founder of the pro-Jacobite *Whirlwind* newspaper. In 1891 he stood as a parliamentary candidate for the Jacobite Individualist Party. He was the only member of this party; he lost the election. At other times he was a Liberal and a Labour supporter. By the 1920s he was heavily flirting with fascism. Jacobites of the left were another part of the revival in the early years. There was a small splinter Jacobite-Legitimist group called the Society of the Red Carnation that fused Christian Socialism with devotion to the Stuarts. Some centrist and left-leaning ideas percolated into nationalist politics in the twentieth century, though Jacobitism was frowned upon by more purist leftists, apart from perhaps by unique iconoclasts such as the Scottish nationalist and communist poet Hugh MacDiarmid.

Back in the Victorian and Edwardian era, the mania for Jacobitism infected two of the leading lights of the occult movement, Samuel Liddell MacGregor Mathers and Aleister Crowley, friends and then rivals in the Golden Dawn society. Though neither had a drop of Scottish blood, they each (at times) adopted a Scottish identity and Mathers even claimed once that he was the reincarnation of King James IV of Scotland. Both also had a fondness for tartan and paraded themselves in full Highland regalia in inappropriate locations. On one occasion in Paris they seem to have absurdly stalked each other while wearing kilts and all associated paraphernalia. In 1911, Crowley published a tract accusing his one-time mentor Mathers of plotting an armed Jacobite rising in Great Britain to replace the monarch. Such a claim was ridiculous and it is doubtful whether there was anyone of rational mind, whether an occultist or not, who considered such a move.

According to the Irish poet W. B. Yeats, Mathers included in his passions a wish to restore Scotland to its former glory, whatever that meant. He may have toyed with the more militant arm of the Legitimist cause that sought to train its members in military technique in preparation for a new revolution to restore the rightful monarchy. Legitimists were active across Europe, seeking to restore what they saw as the rightful royal blood lines for various dispossessed dynasties. In Britain, the movement was a fringe political cause, albeit with shadowy affiliations with more violent bodies, and was proto-fascist in nature. One of the founders of the Order of the White Rose was Bertram, 5th Earl of Ashburnham, who espoused a number of issues including Irish Home Rule and the Spanish Carlist movement which sought to re-establish an alternative Bourbon claimant to the Spanish throne.

Ashburnham trained hopeful Carlist military insurgents on his Welsh estate, though there were never any similar moves to militarise pro-Stuart British legitimists. Beneath the banner of legitimacy Ashburnham was just another upper-class Englishman who thought it his right to interfere in the business of other nations. Late in the nineteenth century he chartered a ship to transport weapons to Spain. The vessel was intercepted; the earl went unpunished. Aleister Crowley was a shadowy participant in these Carlist manoeuvres. Like an after echo of the Jacobite uprisings, Carlist forces had instituted three uprisings in nineteenth-century Spain, all of them failures. Interestingly, the most prominent and militant legitimists were seldom Scottish or Irish. Ashburnham's public Jacobite activities in Great Britain were less sinister than his international aspirations, though he did stir up a whiff of controversy in 1888 when he attempted to have the Church of the Carmelites in London say a full requiem mass for the sake of the soul of Prince Charles Edward Stuart a century after his death. The event was quashed by Cardinal Henry Manning, who felt that such a disloyal ceremony would overcast the reputation of the Roman Catholic Church, which had only recently been able to enjoy full rights in Britain. The event was paralleled by a demonstration at Westminster Abbey in 1892, led by prominent Jacobite the Marquis de Ruvigny. A crowd of 250 gathered with the intention to place wreaths on the tomb of Mary, Queen of Scots. The authorities thought otherwise and police were called to break up the crowd.

Yeats himself, via Mathers and other routes, became emotionally attached to some aspects of Jacobitism and believed that his ancestors had fought on their side at the Battle of the Boyne in 1689. He also claimed kinship with James Butler, 2nd Duke of Ormonde, a key architect in the uprising of 1715 and a subsequent Jacobite alliance with the Swedes. W. B. Yeats was one of the principals of the Celtic Revival, which had profound influence in the arts and culture in all Celtic countries and beyond, lasting to the present. There was a political aspect within the revival, advocating for home rule for the major Celtic nations and, at a more aspirational level, some enthusiasts hoped for a political union of those Celtic countries. For all his potentially dangerous militant ideas Ashburnham, by contrast, proposed an intriguing and plausible federal future for Great Britain, with a relocated capital strangely sited at Chester.

The final embers of the political neo-Jacobite movement died at the outbreak of the First World War. It had always been an oddity to some that ardent British Legitimists wanted to give the British throne to a line of nobility that was resolutely foreign, even more so than the sitting Hanoverian line. The fatal blow was the fact that the current representative of the Stuart line, Crown Prince Rupprecht of Bavaria, awkwardly joined the German army and became an avowed enemy of the United Kingdom. Following the war, continued interest in the Stuarts led to the foundation of two new organisations that supported the cause of the Stuarts, and the cause of monarchy over republicanism, without being overtly politicised. These were the Royal Stuart Society and the Order of the Crown of Stuart, which survive to this day. The political wing of Jacobitism in the Victorian and Edwardian age was always destined to fail because it lacked any clear sense of purpose, let alone politically astute leaders, and the appeal of monarchist legitimism was always going to have a narrow appeal among people with greater concerns in their daily lives. Loyalty to a dynasty that no longer practically existed was always going to be a hard task for the new Jacobites and doomed to fail even harder than their original kindred. If Jacobite politics was a late-Victorian eccentricity, in the twenty-first century it could be classed as a post-modern minority interest heavily dosed with irony. A Scottish Jacobite Party appeared in 2005 and remained active, in a small way, for nearly a decade. Several hundred votes were scraped together in several parliamentary elections but the extremely small political organisation failed to grow. It positioned itself as an alternative to the dominant Scottish National Party but had little historical or philosophical link with what may be called Jacobite concepts. Rather than support a Stuart restoration, or any sort of monarchy, it was avowedly republican in nature and Eurosceptic. Its founder, Dr John Black, slyly linked its counterintuitive name to New Labour, which appeared to be the opposite of 'old' Labour.

Chapter 14
The Sobieski Stuarts

The most conspicuous Jacobites in the nineteenth century were also among the most audacious fakes of the Victorian age and spent decades trying to convince the world they were the descendants of the vanished royal house of Stuart. Living in Scotland, they caused a stir for their claims about their own ancestry and even forged a supposedly ancient book containing the authentic tartans of the Scottish clans. Later, they attracted the attention of people from farther afield.

In the early 1840s, a middle-aged Frenchman began a leisurely journey through the United Kingdom, reversing that trend which saw droves of young affluent British males touring the continent for educational leisure. Charles-Victor Prévot preferred to be known by his adopted aristocratic title of Vicomte d'Arlincourt and his love for self-advancement is significant in light of his description of the Sobieskis. Prévot had made his fortune and found fame by writing several sensational but terribly reviewed bestsellers; he also became an inveterate traveller. He undertook a leisurely journey through the British Isles and Ireland, staying mainly with well-connected families, and wrote an account of his itinerary as *Les Trois Rouyammes* (*The Three Kingdoms*), with a focus on historic places and events, famous people and romantic anecdotes of the past. Scotland, basking in the half-light of its Jacobite afterglow, romantically illuminated by the works of the late Sir Walter Scott, was very much in tune with his tastes.

Staying at Redcastle, at Killearnan in the Black Isle in Scotland, the author heard that Bonnie Prince Charlie had stayed there one night and begged to sleep in the same chamber. At breakfast next day his host, Colonel Baillie, flummoxed the Frenchman by asking whether he had come to the area to meet the Young Pretender's grandchildren. Astonished by the statement, he blurted out what he believed to be common knowledge: that the line of the royal house of Stuart had ended with the death of the cardinal of York in Rome. Not so, his host insisted. There were two brothers who lived on an island nearby who were the handsomest men in the country. They were also the sons of the secret son of Prince Charles Edward Stuart and his wife, Louise the Princess of Stolberg.

The vicomte was soon conducted to the highly romantic abode of the displaced princes, an island belonging to Lord Lovat in the middle of a loch. The situation of the place immediately impressed the French writer:

> This island is a mountain covered with tall trees and pointed rocks, around which foams a circle of waterfalls called Kilmorack. In order to reach this spot, hemmed in by marvels, where the loud voice of the cataract is continually sounding, it is necessary first to cross a light wooden bridge, boldly thrown over abysses and cascades at a fearful height. Then passing among silent defiles and gloomy rocks, we ascend the hill of the Stuarts, and arrive at our journey's end. There, beneath trees a hundred years old, in a solitude where one seems transported a thousand leagues from civilisation, stands a building, the architecture of which is in the style of the middle ages, with ancient windows and painted glass. This strange hermitage, shaded by firs and oaks, has the pediment of a noble mansion, on which are displayed the arms of the Scottish monarchy.

Unfortunately, the princes were not at home on the day of the visit and the vicomte had to be content with a guided tour by one of their wives and her daughter. The story of the princes and, more particularly, their dreamlike abode deeply impressed the visiting writer. And yet, this historical fantasist stopped short of actually admitting belief in their fairytale. 'I do not judge, I relate,' he stated coyly about the brothers.

Who were these two men who claimed to embody the last vestiges of the royal Stuart bloodline? They were, above all, products of their own time. The Victorian age spawned many strange individuals entranced by the past who fulfilled their romantic fantasies to the extent of actually living most of their lives in the guise of figures from their favourite eras, or successors to vanished dynasties. Fewer in number are those figures who convinced others that they were the legitimate heirs of historical figure. Two such men were the Sobieski Stuart brothers. They began life quite mundanely as John Carter Allen and Charles Manning Allen and later concocted the fantasy that they were the sole descendants of Bonnie Prince Charlie. They may have come to believe this deception themselves, for they not only created an audacious and detailed backstory but also claimed to be custodians of national dress, expertly cataloguing Scottish Highland tartans, which were in fact bogus but so audaciously done they remain the foundation of the modern tartan industry.

The brothers' father was a low-ranking English naval officer named Thomas Allen. They claimed that Thomas was actually the secret son of Prince Charles Edward Stuart and his wife Louise, despite the fact that this famously tempestuous couple had no children. The family legend stated that Thomas was secretly smuggled into England and adopted by his actual father, admiral John Carter Allen. The fantasy version has Prince Charles Edward entrusting his secret, only begotten heir to the care of the admiral, fearful that the evil British establishment would hunt down and kill the boy. Prior to the more daring claim to represent the last descendants of the Stuart monarchy, some members of the Allen family attempted to claim affiliation with a lesser Scottish noble line, the Hay Earls of Errol, but this link seems counterfeit too. Facts about the background of the brothers are vague. The elder future royal pretender John Carter Allen was born in Wales in the late eighteenth century and Charles Manning Allen was probably born in Oxfordshire a few years later. The Allen brothers had an obscure upbringing but in early adulthood associated themselves with Scotland and were immersing themselves in its Highland culture, as well as seeking patronage from nobles such as the Duke of Argyll and Earl of Moray. By the 1830s the siblings were styling themselves as grandsons of the Young Pretender. Before they fully adopted their royal personas, they subtly adapted their names and styled themselves as John Hay Alan and Charles Stuart Hay Alan. They used various aliases during their lives, including the surname Owen, as well as occasionally altering their family name from Allen to Alan. While researching their pedigree and tartan history, they lived in several residences near Inverness. Their backstory impressed Thomas Fraser, 12th Lord Lovat, enough to build a hunting lodge for them on Eilean Aigas, near Beauly, where they moved to in 1838. Like Lovat, the brothers were now also Catholics, which they saw as an integral component of their highly royalist, Jacobite personas. The island incidentally had once been the headquarters of the notorious sometime Jacobite rogue Simon Fraser, 11th Lord Lovat.

John and Charles claimed that their true descent from the exiled house of Stuart was revealed to them around 1811. An early component of their self-mythologising involved them also claiming that they had served in the French army during his campaigns and had fought at several battles, including Waterloo. Their own legend states that the Emperor Napoleon himself heard about these two royal Stuart princelings and drew them to his service. On the battlefield, he took the cross from his own uniform and presented it to John Sobieski. Another whispered rumour says that the emperor contemplated displacing the Hanovers again from their imperial throne in Great Britain and replacing them with their rightfully royal brothers. One of Napoleon's successors, King Charles X of France (who reigned 1824–30), was also said to have been impressed with the credentials of the Allen brothers; at least, according to the story they bandied about.

The siblings' later claims to be the custodians of the formal history of clan tartans in Scotland began to emerge in the late 1820s, when the brothers started claiming that they had access to a manuscript based on a work compiled in the 1570s by the Scottish Catholic historian John Leslie, Bishop of Ross, which was a comprehensive collection of the official and authentic tartans worn by many Scottish families, both in the Gaelic north of the nation and the Lowlands. This dubious source found its way, according to the Allens, into the library of the Scots College at Douai in France, and there into the hands of Bonnie Prince Charlie, who passed it down to them as a precious family heirloom. Authorities were immediately divided about the authenticity of this document. Many in Scotland properly pointed out the fact that territorial and clan tartans were in no way codified at any point in history, a fact emphasised by Sir Walter Scott and others. There is some irony in the ire of Sir Walter quite rightly protesting that Lowland families never wore tartan when he was responsible for the cynical tartanisation of Edinburgh during the royal visit of King George IV in 1822. Hearing about the claims of the Allens to be in possession of the tartan holy grail, Scott had demanded to see this so-called antiquarian manuscript that the brothers claimed was in their possession. Their response, through an intermediary, was evasive. But the publication of their book detailing the Highland and Lowland tartans was notably long delayed, until after Sir Walter was dead and buried. Others who later asked to see the original manuscript were presented with an eighteenth-century copy that the brothers claimed was derived from the sixteenth-century original.

John Allen, by now calling himself John Sobieski Stuart (honouring not only the last Stuart pretender but also his maternal Polish descent), published the monumental book *Vestiarum Scoticum* in Edinburgh in 1842. The work arrived as a very limited edition work and contained a written description of more than seventy 'historic' tartans. One authority on tartan weaving, Mr James Scarlett, pointedly noted that the tartans seemed to have been designed on a drawing board rather than a loom. Yet many people, including enthusiastic clan chiefs hungry to rekindle their diminished heritage, seized upon the 'authorised' patterns designs for the kilts supposedly worn by their ancestors in the misty past. It has to be admitted, authenticity aside, that the designs were highly accomplished and acted as a template for tartan design down to the present day.

Their claims to be custodians of this Highland tradition was bolstered in the following year by *The Costumes of The Clans*, an even more sumptuous volume, composed by both brothers. A modern historian, Trevor Roper, has paid respect to the huge amount of effort and wide-ranging sources that went into this book, even though the wider (and wilder) claims of the brothers are discredited. Despite support from eminent Scots such as the publisher Robert Chambers, there was widespread opposition to their ideas about their fantasy version of Highland dress and culture. Undaunted by this, the brothers published other works, including short fiction for periodicals. Both had turned their hands to poetry; some of which was set to music by others, and later themselves. A notable work appeared in 1847, authored by the two men under the names John Sobieski Stuart and Charles Edward Stuart. This work was titled *Tales of the Century* and contained the adventures of an ardent Jacobite nicknamed *Iolair Dhearg*, the Red Eagle. The book sold itself as a barely fictionalised account of the brothers' own supposedly Jacobite Stuart background.

But who were these men and why were so many people ready to give credence to their claims? Scotland was a nation peculiarly separated from its own sense of statehood in the nineteenth century and vulnerable to spurious attempts to assert its ancient identity. Those who supported the fading Gaelic institutions were sometimes lauded, despite their often-odd versions of history. The Allen brothers apparently had some charm and star quality that enabled them to carry off their deceptions with lords and commoners alike. Habitually bedecked in full Highland attire, the brothers cut dashing figures right from their initial appearance in Scotland and were conspicuous at balls and social events in the Highlands. In London too, the pseudo royals also caused a stir. On one occasion, an awestruck Scottish servant announced the arrival of the 'preences' at an artist's studio and all present dropped to their knees in the presence of the 'last of the Stuarts'. When they attended an event at the Chelsea Hotel, many of those present remarked on the likeness of the two young brothers to the dispossessed Stuart royals. Their handsome faces, dignified bearing and air of melancholy detachment were much admired and taken as evidence of their royal descent. Back in Scotland, the young James Thomson met the siblings when they visited his native district in 1829 and was somewhat dazzled by their Jacobite auras. He wore a coin given by one of them against his breast and it became a burning romantic token linked to his hopes that the rightful Stuart monarchy would one day return. Thomson and many others in Scotland were affected by the rosy afterglow of the Jacobite uprising. He would have fought for them, had he been alive at the time, but in his maturity he admitted that the adherence to this aspect of the past, which the Sobieski brothers so successfully represented, faded away during the reign of Queen Victoria. Seen as an adult he eventually realised that the figurehead, Bonnie Prince Charlie himself, was 'devoid of all virtues that make even poor men great'.

The folklore collector John Francis Campbell of Islay noted that he did not believe in the strict demarcation of clan tartans that the Sobieski

Stuarts and other promoted and avowed late in life that he could not, as a scholar, accept their *Vestiarium Scoticum* as a credible work, though they had been his friends for half a century. A pen portrait of the brothers was composed by Elizabeth Grant of Rothiemurchus, who first encountered the two men in the mid-1820s. She stated that their sudden claim to be royal Stuarts astonished their own father. Their mother, she said, was Scottish and had been in the service of the exiled Stuarts in Italy. Perhaps this is where their outlandish origin story came from. Her picture of the pseudo royals in their Highland home remains a compelling snapshot of the highly romantic, slightly deluded atmosphere in which their whole family lived:

> [The brothers] were handsome men, particularly John Sobieski, who, however, had not a trace of the Stuart in his far finer face. They always wore the Highland dress, kilt and belted plaid, and looked melancholy, and spoke at times mysteriously. The effect they produced was astonishing; they were 'feted' to their hearts' content; half the Clans actually believed in them; for several years they actually 'reigned' in the north country. At last they made a mistake which finished the farce.
>
> Fraser of Lovat had taken them up enthusiastically, built them a villa on an island in the Beauly Firth, in the pretty garden of which was a small waterfall. Here Mrs Charles Stuart sat and played the harp like Flora MacIvor, and crowds went to visit them. They turned Roman Catholic, to please their benefactor, I suppose, and so lost caste with the public. Poor Mrs Charles was a meek little woman, a widow with a small jointure whom the 'prince', her husband, had met in Ireland. I do not know what had taken him there, for no one knew what his employment had originally been. Prince Sobieski had been a coach painter – not the panel painter, the heraldic painter – and most beautifully he finished the coats of arms.

The brothers were largely self-educated and were proficient in several languages. They were enthusiastic and successful in field sports and, more unusually, were adept artisans in several crafts. As well as being heraldic painters, the Sobieskis were skilled wood carvers and furniture makers. If it was not for the stupendous claims about their own lineage, they would have been fine examples of the multiskilled and energetic individuals who flourished in nineteenth-century Great Britain. One of their foremost supporters was the author Sir Thomas Dick Lauder, who corresponded with Walter Scott about them. He admired the great store of knowledge that John and Charles Allen possessed, though he thought it had been 'gobbled up at random'. The great problem was their lack of education and the fact that they were actually woefully ignorant in most matters. The overarching deceit about tartan history and their own ancestors was all consuming, and it is difficult to tell now how genuine they were in their own convictions. The Scottish ancestry of the brothers' mother, mentioned by Elizabeth Grant, seems like yet another Allen family falsehood, for most accounts state that her name was Manning and she was the daughter of a vicar from Surrey. The extent to which the brothers' father shared or even inspired the delusion of royal Stuart birth is questionable. He seems to have at least believed that he was connected with the noble line of the earls of Errol. He had several illegitimate children who migrated to Scotland and adopted the surname MacGaradh. For much of his life he covered his tracks and took on a variety of other names to hide from creditors.

The brothers' later years were not marked by success. Growing disdain and scepticism about their personal claims of royal ancestry and their claims regarding tartans meant they were no longer taken seriously in some circles. Some sources assert that they went abroad for nearly twenty years, sometimes residing (or pretending to reside) at Versailles, but more often at the Bohemian royal palace in Prague. They were living in London in the late 1860s and were amiable and eccentric fixtures of the reading room of the British Library, where it was noted that they kindly assisted visiting novice researchers. One who saw them there was R. C. Francillon, and he had decidedly negative views on the older Allen sibling. John, he wrote, displayed an 'air of melancholy dignity – no professional actor could have bettered the part of a dethroned king; his picturesque costume, frogged and furred, the more pathetically effective for the apparent length of its wear'. The supposed prince's knowledge of Latin grammar was, furthermore, appalling.

By this stage, it was clear that they absolutely believed their own myth, even if it's uncertain whether this was true when they were younger men. One of the books they were hopefully working on at this period was the never-published but aptly named *Illustrations of Popular Delusions*. John grandly designated himself as 'the chevalier John Sobieski Stewart', and in the 1870s was adopting the mock Franco-Scottish title Count d'Albanie. John died in London in February 1872 and his brother Charles adopted the Albany title and died in France in 1880. John and Charles were buried at Eskadale in their beloved Highlands. John's inscription commemorates him as John Sobieski Stuart, Count d'Albanie.

Through good fortune, Charles's son Charles Edward Stuart Allen married Alice Hay, daughter of the Earl of Errol, the Scottish noble family from which the Allens falsely claimed descent. The couple had no children and died in the early 1880s, so this shadow line of the royal Stuarts itself became extinct. Towards the ends of their lives the Sobieski Stuarts were living in poverty or very near it. The brothers did not benefit from the huge boom in the tartan industry that they began. Other authors wrote their own descriptive volumes on clan tartans based on the *Vestiarum* and achieved far greater success. The biggest winners in the matter were weavers and Highland outfitters. Back in the beginning, Walter Scott wondered whether the brothers' claims concerning the kilt was actually a conspiracy sponsored by weavers of tartan cloth. They have benefitted from the business ever since. In modern times, the most notable focus on the Sobieski Stuarts has been a demolition of their claims by the English historian Hugh Trevor-Roper (one of those who had been originally duped by the forged Hitler diaries). His book, *The Invention of Scotland*, serves as a well-written, wholesale demolition of much of the historical myths of the Scottish nation. In terms of literary output, the Sobieskis' works are forgotten as artistic endeavours. The fraud they perpetrated with tartanising their adoptive homeland came several generations after the fraudulent Ossian poems of James Macpherson that purported to be productions of the remote Gaelic past.

The Sobieski princes are major figures in the strange afterglow world of the Jacobites in the nineteenth century. The lives of fantasists frequently beget ongoing bursts of fresh fantasy long after their passing. So, the Canadian author Nadine Mackenzie claimed that the lack of facts about the early life of Charles Allen suggested that he and John were unrelated and, in fact, secret lovers. It is ironic that they succeeded in making many others believe their claims of descent from Charles Edward Stuart while their early contemporary Count Roehenstart, who really was a descendant, struggled to convince others. There may have been a time indeed when Roehenstart and the Sobieskis were resident at the same time in different parts of Scotland. The count though may not have been aware of them immediately, for the only record of him objecting to their false claims seems to date from the 1830s.

Some modern theories have continued to peck away at the inscrutable Allen brothers' real family history. The author Hugh Douglas has reignited the debate by circulating the possibility that the Sobieskis may indeed have been descended from the Young Pretender, but through a secret child he had with his mistress Marie Louise, Duchess de Montbazon. She had a son named Charles Godfrey in 1748, who people believed to have been fathered by her husband. The infant died some months later; so the story goes. But there was a rumour that something else happened. Napoleon heard the gossip and had the child's coffin opened and found it was empty. The legend states that the boy was brought to Great Britain and was given the conspicuous name Charles Stuart (hardly a guarantee of anonymity) and raised under the wings of the Erroll family. He allegedly died in 1820. The story is nonsense.

The Sobieski brothers succeeded through a combination of charm and industry, churning out a stream of romantic Jacobite propaganda to serve their claims. They are also, more legitimately, descendants of a long line of pretenders (an ironic title in their context); mostly men who falsely claimed, and may have largely believed, that they were the long-lost representatives of royal lines deprived of their rightful inheritance. Another eccentric and deluded royal Jacobite descendant was George Henry de Strabolgie Neville Plantagenet Harrison, author of a dubious history of Yorkshire in the late Victorian age. He was notable for claiming descent from the god Odin and also that he was the rightful Duke of Lancaster. This psychological condition survived into the twentieth century. One well-known sufferer was a Shropshire policeman named Anthony William Hall, who convinced himself (and no one else) that he was a legitimate male-line descendant of King Henry VIII.

Chapter 15

The Polish Connection and Other Overseas Stuarts

While the history of the Jacobites is most associated with the British Isles, exile after the failed rebellions and subsequent emigration have ensured that the echoes of the movement have been felt in some distant places, not least those parts of the world that became part of the British empire. In the early years of the twentieth century, inspired by the memories of Roehenstart and the false Sobieski brothers, there were other rumours of the survival of the bloodline of Bonnie Prince Charlie. These wisps may have also been given credence by the popular fallacy about the survival of the last tsar's daughter Anastasia that was widespread in the mid-twentieth century.

In the 1930s there was a minor resurgence of interest in the ill-fortuned Baron Roehenstart. A story that was circulated during the period stated that Roehenstart was once desperate to claim his rightful family inheritance and asked his sister, Marie Stuart Roehenstart, who was living in Warsaw, to provide family documents to prove his lineage. His sister did not want to send these important papers that had belonged to her grandmother, so she travelled to Scotland where her brother was residing. She then booked travel back to Poland on board a Dundee whaler ship. But, unfortunately, the ship's captain, William Stewart, was a rogue and abducted her, stealing the family documents that were in a conspicuous gold box. Not content with this, the villainous whaler stranded the unfortunate lady on desolate Campbell Island in New Zealand, where she unhappily perished.

One version of the story was published in the *Oban Times* in 1939. It stated that the Young Pretender's daughter Charlotte, Duchess of Albany, married a Swedish Baron Roehenstart and had two children who were afterwards concealed and adopted by a noble family. Marie Stuart married a Pole named James Sobieski, and they had issue. This Polish connection has some truth in it at least, as shall be seen later in this chapter.

But what of the exiled Marie living on uninhabited Campbell Island? Local legend, hopelessly entangled with melodramatic period literature, says that a romantic lived here around 1810. The island lies 700 kilometres south of New Zealand's South Island and 270 kilometres south-east of the Auckland Islands and is the very epitome of remoteness. Still, the land managed to keep her in solitude somehow, occasionally spotted by passing vessels, 'tripping along the shores of Campbell Island wearing Stuart tartan, paisley shawl, shoes with silver buckles, and in her glengarry bonnet, a sprig of Scottish heather'. One tradition has the evil captain Stewart contrarily building the enforced exile a hut that he stocked with provisions, along with a bell that she could ring to mark the Angelus during her solitary hours. In the decades since the death of this mysterious lady, her grave was often pointed out, and can still be seen marked by an iron cross. Also remaining are the foundations of her earthen hut near Camp Cove. There is a spurious story that the grave was opened in the mid-twentieth century and revealed a skeleton clutching a silver crucifix and with a ring on its finger with the Stuart clan crest.

According to contrasting traditions, Stewart either kidnapped the unfortunate girl from Le Havre in France, or he agreed to transport her far away, to safeguard her from dastardly British agents. But the pair fell out and he sold her to a sealing crew who marooned her. Whatever the details, her fate was inevitable: sealers visiting the place a few years later found her skeleton, with its fingers pathetically clutching a sprig of ancestral Scottish heather. A variant of the colourful tale names the royal Stuart lady as Marie Almand. Her story inspired two novels: *The Lady of the Heather* (1945) by Australian Will Lawson and *Marie Levant* (1913) by New Zealander Carlyle Ferguson, though the earliest literary interest in the tale was stirred up in the 1890s by a journalist named Robert Carrick. Literary invention is stamped over all the florid versions of the story. Variants on the tale are not burdened by fact and checkable information, and wildly contradict each other. One source says the lady of the heather was actually the granddaughter of Flora MacDonald, the iconic Jacobite heroine. Another account insists she was a Hanoverian spy exiled on Campbell Island by Jacobites. Yet another variation states that she was the granddaughter of King Louis XVII of France but had a Scottish mother. The whole tangle of tales was inspired by a real-life tragedy involving another young lady. She was Elizabeth Farr (or Parr), the young Irish-Australian mistress of a sea captain, who was drowned in an accident along with him and several others in late 1810. Sir James Clark Ross visited the island in 1840 and reported several lonely graves there, including that of a French woman who had been drowned there.

Inevitably, a mournful ghostly lady has sometimes been seen in the vicinity. The lady of Campbell Island was seen by two sailors from the ship *Amokura* who spent a night there in 1907. One of them, Harry Chapelle, related:

> I couldn't get to sleep and when I looked through the small window of our hut, I saw two bright eyes staring in at me. I woke Reg and we went outside, and in the moonlight, saw the form of a woman in a shawl making her way to the top of the rise. We followed, carefully avoiding the cliff edge. The wild sea roared in the darkness below us. As we passed the grave, a long piercing scream rent the air and the macabre figure disappeared.

If New Zealand is far from the sphere of the historical Jacobites, then Italy was at its epicentre for some time. The exiled Stuart court in Rome was fatally undermined by the effective intelligence machine of the British government whose spies feverishly unearthed its secrets. The exiled royals were also subject to the other political currents that swirled around the papal see. They had their own ghosts to contend with. Not least of these were the physical reminders of the profligacy of their own recent ancestors. Various rumours that there were descendants of the British Stuarts, spawned from illegitimate children, persisted through the centuries.

Among the Stuart bastards, one of the most prominent was Don Giocomo Stuardo. He had the honour and perhaps misfortune to be the son of the first illegitimate son of King Charles II, according to some. Don Giocomo was born in 1669, son of Jacques (or James) de la Cloche du Bourg de Jersey (who apparently died shortly before his birth) and possibly a lady named Marguerite de Carteret who was married to a man named Jean de la Cloche. Legend states that his royal father had a liaison with this married lady when he was just 16. Despite his Catholic religion and his Italian nationality, Giocomo seemed convinced that he could one day become king of Great Britain. In this circumstance he was not so different from the legitimate Pretenders, Old and Young.

Unlike other progeny born out of royal wedlock, for some reason Jacques was only recognised by his father in private. Royal bastards could be problematic for legitimate rulers. Another child of Charles II, the Duke of Monmouth, was executed for rebelling against his uncle, James II. James Francis, the Old Pretender, was subject to false accusations that he himself was not royal, but a non-royal who was smuggled into his mother's maternity bed in a warming pan. This untruth was gleefully circulated by Whigs for years after his birth. James Francis may have felt he had trouble enough with existing family members – both his half-sisters stole his crown – without troubling himself with any more unwanted relatives.

Jacques lived in various parts of Europe and briefly became a Jesuit. He was given written, secret assurance that he could claim high title if ever he returned to England, which he did not have the opportunity to fulfil. The truth of his heritage was detailed in several documents that remained hidden in the Church archives for many years. His son was possibly aware of this correspondence, which spurred on his own high ambition. A person naming himself James (or Giacopo) Stuart and claiming to be the son of the English king appeared in Naples in 1669. He may have been Jacques or someone else appropriating his identity. One theory is that he was a French servant of the real Jacques who stole his papers and perhaps even murdered him. A rumour also circulated in Naples that he was the secret son or perhaps child of the king of Denmark. He was thrown into prison but was released and went to Venice where he died soon afterwards.

Don Giocomo spent all his life in Italy. In July 1718 he contacted the exiled James Edward Stuart in Rome. James was then unmarried and may have looked unlikely to continue the Stuart royal line, which may have raised Giocomo's ambition for recognition. Stuardo was seeking, firstly, acknowledgment of his own royal heritage and financial support, a request that the exiled king may have felt unwilling to concede due to his own straitened circumstances. Like the shadow of a shadow, Stuardo lived a furtive life, though he seems to have inherited some wealth from his father. Due to the intricacies of European dynastic politics, he had to live incognito in Naples for several decades. He may have stepped from the shadows too soon, for in 1711 he was charged with being an imposter claiming to be grandson of King Charles II. After a year-long proceeding, he was triumphantly recognised in his claim. However, in an echo of the later fate of Baron Roehenstart, his fortune was mysteriously removed. His homes in Naples were appropriated by others; his money in the banks was frozen. It's likely that his own characteristics played some part in his downfall, for he was described at the time as lacking in both intelligence and money.

Despite setbacks, Stuardo did not go away or immediately fall back into obscurity. He cultivated a series of influential friends, enough to ensure that he could avoid poverty even if his status was still precarious. In May 1736 he appealed again to the Old Pretender, mentioning their common lineage as well as offering to show certificates that proved his identity. He voiced his extreme need in his letter and beseeched James to send him an answer, 'not only as a consolation for my pains, but to glorify my Stuart blood'.

James Francis Stuart decided it would be unwise to have much to do with a supposed royal cousin, which seems ironic in light of the fact that one of his closest friends and supporters was the 2nd Duke of Berwick, another descendant of royalty whose father had been illegitimate, albeit he had the good fortune to be publicly recognised. Despite the formal rebuff, Berwick seems to have been instructed by James to examine the burial condition of Giacomo's father in Naples and order a formal funeral in 1736 or 1737. Berwick himself died in 1738. Stuardo wrote again to the Old Pretender in 1739, with the same lack of response. By a strange turn of events, the 3rd Duke of Berwick decided to change his family surname from FitzJames to Stuardo, in an echo of his unrecognised distant relative. This caused family uproar until the surname was altered by compromise to FitzJames-Stuardo.

In 1743, the now elderly Stuardo faced the indignity of being arrested again as a royal imposter, this time in Rome, and he was deported to Naples. He went through the rigours of legal process to hire lawyers and produce a manifesto that supported his own royal claims, and it gained some sympathy when it was circulated, though silence continued from the official exiled royal Stuart kindred. The lack of response from the exiled Jacobite family may have been caused by the fact they were still fighting off the false 'warming pan' story that insisted King James III was in fact a base-born imposter. After some years in poverty, it seems that he died some little while after this, in the early 1750s.

Less than a sad footnote in the history, the Italian Stuarts are still something of an unresolved mystery. It has been claimed that the father and son were not descended from royalty and letters that supposedly came from the king were forgeries. There are certainly questions to be asked about their origins. One popular story insists that Jacques was actually imprisoned for life in order to silence the truth of his relationship to the Stuarts, giving rise to the fable of the Man in the Iron Mask. (A Jacobite twist on the legend of the Man in the Iron Mask says that the mysterious prisoner was an English nobleman who was mixed up in a plot of the Duke of Berwick to overthrow King William III. This fable appeared as early as 1711, soon after the mysterious masked man had died.)

Another complication arises from the incognito that Charles II allegedly once advised to adopt when travelling: Henri de Rohan. This name eerily prefigures the connection with the French family of that name and Baron Roehenstart. Some writers state that Giacomo had a son named Giuseppe or Joseph (1722–83), who supposedly fought alongside Prince Charles Edward Stuart in the '45 and even came back on the same ship with him to France in 1746. He later acted as a double of Prince Charles Edward while the latter was absent on secret missions.

Giuseppe later settled at Kilvala in Brittany. A tale says that Joseph had a son named Augustus Edward (alias Ferdinand Smyth-Stuart) who married the Young Pretender's daughter Charlotte and himself became father of the boy who became Baron Roehenstart. Another myth connects him with the family of Napoleon. The Italian Stuarts are mentioned by Michael Lafosse in his book *The Forgotten Monarchy of Scotland*, but his text only reiterates misinformation about the family. These tortuous legends are almost certainly untrue. But the real history of the Stuardos may never be disentangled. Even the perceptive Victorian and Edwardian writer Andrew Lang could not get to the truth of these shadow Stuarts. The family likely petered out in parallel with the legitimate exiled Stuart branch, though there may have been some genuine offshoots in Italy. A lady who claimed to be the daughter of the Old Pretender may have died in 1797. Not all the Stuarts in Italy, however, were descended from royalty. Manuel Stuart, who settled in Corsica in 1766, had been a Jacobite-sympathising member of the Royal Navy who deserted and settled in Italy in the previous decade. Various families in Italy claimed to be Stuarts and some claiming a relationship with the British royal family survived the Victorian age. Alice Shield, writing in 1908, noted that, 'One constantly hears up and down Italy of this and that insignificant person claiming to be "the last of the Stuarts". Even a family named Sindari hint that they might translate their name to Stewart and claim royal kin!'

The dukes of Berwick, as we have seen, represented another line of descent from the last Stuart kings. James FitzJames, 1st Duke of Berwick (1670–1734), was son of King James VII and II and became an accomplished figure in the king's civil and military service. He followed his royal father into exile and fought on his behalf in Ireland and later served with huge distinction as a military leader under Louis XIV, commanding the Wild Geese of Irish military exiles as well as others. He was reckoned one of the top military commanders in Europe. The French created him Duke of FitzJames while he also gained the Spanish title Duke of Liria.

Although committed to the family Jacobite cause, FitzJames and his half-brother James Francis Stewart did not always see eye to eye. The Old Pretender recognised his sibling's military skills and importance in the run-up to the proposed Jacobite uprising in 1715, but he was frustrated in his attempts to persuade Berwick to head the venture. Berwick had become a French citizen in 1704 and, as the French state did not officially support the Jacobites, declined to participate. The French regent, the Duc d'Orléans, refused him permission to leave France and James angrily thought his half-brother was responsible for turning the regent against the expedition. He frustratingly described Berwick as being 'incommunicable and Incomprehensible' on the matter. When Berwick directly stated that he refused the Pretender's commission to lead troops to invade Scotland, his brother furiously wrote that he would never again ask for favours from 'a disobedient subject and bastard'. It was a bitter retort to an older brother whom he had worshipped in his formative years. Berwick had otherwise always been outspoken in his advice to his brother and usually counselled him with good sense. Few could risk being as blunt with the king as he could. When the Old Pretender's ailing sister Anne was reigning as queen of Great Britain, Berwick advised James to go to London and throw himself on her mercy in the hope that she would declare him her heir and the Stuart dynasty would continue. It was not in James's nature to take such a risk, even though he had little to lose. Berwick could not prevail against the pessimistic hesitancy of his half-brother, especially as his own character was far more dynamic than James Francis's. Recognising his headstrong nature, the queen of Spain described him as, 'A great dry devil of an Englishman who always goes his own way'.

James FitzJames lived until 1734, but his relationship with the Old Pretender never fully recovered. But the head of the Stuart dynasty became close instead to Berwick's son, James Francis, the Duke of Liria, whose friendly and compliant manner was in contrast to the more forthright qualities of his father. The Berwicks became French Ducs de Fitz James and Spanish Ducques de Liria and of Alba. The Spanish line survives to the present and this shadow Jacobite family follows a more clearly defined succession than the supposedly legitimate Jacobite succession that was descended through a tortuous series of twists and turns in various family trees. The FitzJames-Stuardo lineage avoided the historical mantrap that James II and his male descendants succumbed to by realising that a return to British rule was a forlorn hope. By refusing to be shackled to their roots, they were able to flourish elsewhere in Europe, and could be seen as a truer embodiment of the royal Stuart heritage supposedly represented by various disinterested dukes of Bavaria and their kindred.

One important aspect of the history of the royal Stuarts and the Jacobites that has crucial bearing on both their background and their legacy is their connection with Poland. This link is rarely explored in histories of the dynasty or works on the Jacobites, yet it has significance in any assessment of this hapless royal family. While the Stuarts were mediocre as political and military leaders, the maternal heritage of the Pretenders could claim to be more dazzling. James Francis Stuart married Maria Clementina Sobieska, whose grandfather was John III Sobieski, king of Poland from 1674 to 1696. Contemporaries of the Pretenders occasionally made reference to the greatness of their eastern European maternal ancestry, but the military genius from that heritage did not manifest in them. There were suggestions that James II should be offered the elective throne of Poland following his ignominious expulsion from Great Britain, after John Sobieski's death, which would have been a solution to his embarrassing exile and was much favoured by Louis XIV of France. Not only would it remove the ex-British king from French territory and thus clear the way for unfettered diplomacy with the new British rulers; it would also maintain French influence in Poland. A prince of royal blood and a fervent Catholic, and moreover someone who had nothing to do with entitled factions in Poland, there was much to recommend James for the role. Poland also had historical connections with Scotland, through a substantial population of Scottish merchants in the country stretching back into the early sixteenth century, plus a stream of Scots seeking military employment there. But James ruled out a bid for the Polish crown because it would be tantamount to him turning his back on recovering the British throne, and also because the Polish crown was not hereditary, he would leave his son James Francis without a kingdom.

John Sobieski was an extremely prominent member of the aristocracy in Poland and a leading figure in the pro-French faction in his country. He was elected to the kingship and led extensive military campaigns even into his final years despite his failing health. His greatest victory was leading a coalition of European forces against a massive Ottoman Empire army at the Battle of Vienna in 1683, a decisive battle that finally terminated the threat of further Turkish expansion on the continent. He was lauded by the pope and feted by other figures as the saviour of Western Europe and Christendom.

King John's wife, and maternal great-grandmother of the Stuart princes, was Marie Casimire (Marysienka), a native French noblewoman who became an influential character in Rome after her husband's death, though she died in France in 1716. Her figure may have reminded the princes Charles Edward and Henry of their other royal heritage, though Marie was not a universally popular figure in Rome because of her austere arrogance. Her son James Sobieski was active in France and Poland and suffered the consequences of allowing his daughter Marie Clementina Sobieska to marry the exiled Stuart Prince James Edward, losing the favour of the Holy Roman Emperor who was in alliance with Great Britain. Marie had been imprisoned in Innsbruck to prevent her journeying to marry James Edward, but in June 1719 she was dramatically freed by an Irish-led mission that liberated her and transported her to Italy through enemy territory. If possibly not the highlight of her life, it was its most dramatic episode and her high hopes of a regally splendid existence in Rome were dashed by reality. James Edward Stuart was a passive, pedestrian husband, the Stuart court was a shadow player in the papal capital, and there was insufficient money to maintain a magnificent lifestyle that she initially expected. Despite evident difficulties between the couple, James Sobieski tried to advance the interests of his son-in-law, suggesting that he should advance himself as a candidate for the monarchy of Poland. With his eye still on the receding throne of Britain, James Edward demurred but suggested that his younger son Henry might be considered a suitable alternative candidate. 'The blood of the Sobieskis runs in his veins,' James Stuart wrote fancifully, 'and by what may be judged of a child of such tender years, he will not be unworthy of it.' Thankfully, for Poland and for Henry too, the plan never came to fruition. Similar plans for Charles Edward after Culloden also fell through.

James Sobieski attempted to give his Stuart grandsons access to their Polish birthright, negotiating support with the Russian empress in 1734 so that Charles and Henry could undergo the legal process of *indygenat*, which allowed foreign nobles to enter the ranks of Polish-Lithuanian aristocracy. But his plan ended with his own death in 1737, two years after the untimely demise of his daughter. Marie Sobieska had retreated into religion while keeping a needlessly jealous eye on females she thought were too keenly interested in her husband. Her ascetic lifestyle, allied with morbid disappointment, hastened her early death in 1735, leaving both her boys bereft. Her religious vehemence left its influence on Henry especially, though hardly on Charles Edward. But her post-mortem saintliness (if it was such) added to the pious aura that some believed the Stuarts possessed. Living in a convent, she devoted her final days to the poor and was reckoned a saint by the local people and priests, and the aura lingered. It was noted that a Polish noblewoman's child was cured of a putrid fever through her direct afterlife intervention.

Prince Charles Edward continued to have sporadic connections with Polish individuals throughout his life. One of his few mistresses was Marie-Anne de la Trémouille, Princess de Talmont, a distant cousin of his mother's side, whose father was the Polish nobleman Count Jablonowski, a relation of Queen Marie Leczinsca of France. Like all his intimate relationships, this liaison did not last or end amicably. Another link with the Poles was Charles's friendship with Bishop Joesph Zaluski, with whom he corresponded for decades. In one of his letters Charles advised that Poland 'will always be dear and respected' by him, even though he had never visited the homeland of his maternal ancestors. Most of the Poles the Stuarts and Jacobites associates encountered were also exiles, mostly resident in France, and only one of a cosmopolitan continental circle of aristocracy that interacted with each other.

One of the most intriguing Polish characters on the fringes of the Jacobite world was the diplomat and soldier Count Stanisław Poniatowski, a trusted associate of Swedish King Charles XII. Half-Jewish, he also had Stuart as well as Polish blood in his veins and was particularly active in freemasonry and plotted with Jacobites and sympathisers in Sweden, France, Russia and elsewhere, particularly around the time of the 1715 rebellion. Around 1750, Charles Edward was also in close contact with Stanislaus Leszczyński, one-time monarch of Poland, who now had a large estate in France at Lunéville, and who was as deeply involved in freemasonry as the Stuart prince allegedly was. He was also the father-in-law of King Louis XV and had impeccable social connections across Europe. However, despite his willingness, he was not successful in gaining support for Charles Edward with either his French connections or with the Hapsburg Empress Marie Theresa, who had expressed sympathy with restoring the exiled Stuarts. The latter was cultivated, through the

Franco-Pole and via other contacts made by Murray of Elibank, but again the frenetic scheming of Jacobite exiles came to nothing. When Charles Edward disappeared from view in August 1771, the British government were frantic for information on his whereabouts. Domestic rumours said that he was skulking around the Scottish Highlands. In Europe, it was reported that the elusive prince was in Poland and was assisting nationalists there in their struggle against Russian aggression, a rumour that was believed plausible, though it was untrue. There had been rumours of the prince heading to Poland as early as 1749, according to a Colonel Yorke who wrote to the secretary of state in London. Many Poles were dissatisfied with their ruler August II of Poland and III of Saxony, who was an ally of Hanoverian Britain. Charles's Sobieski connection may have been sought by a faction in that nation; London was distantly perturbed. There were also whispers that Charles Edward was seeking to venture to Poland to seek marriage with a member of the distinguished Radziwill family. Reports of Charles briefly visiting Poland in 1753, on his way to Russia, seem to have been a deliberately false trail.

The Stuart royal family also benefitted materially from their Polish connection, having a share in the fortune that was part of the Sobieski legacy. Money, jewels and other heirlooms were split between the descendants of King John, though the Stuarts had to fight at times for what they believed was their rightful share. Prince James Sobieski died in 1737 and the Stuarts expected a significant share of his estate, but it was not all secured, because other Sobieski connections disputed the fortune, primarily the Duchess of Bouillon and her family. Within the family, there was also squabbling about the inheritance. In his last years, Prince Charles hoped to obtain two large Sobieski rubies for his daughter the Duchess of Albany but his brother Henry, who had long experience of his financial waywardness, refused to hand them over.

Poland was also seen as a possible refuge for some prominent Jacobites, possibly because it was seen as being remote and therefore hopefully free of British spies and paid men who were rife in France and Italy. General Lord George Murray fell foul of the Young Pretender for supposed disobedience during the '45 and was never forgiven by the prince. He was received with honour by the Old Pretender in Rome but struggled like a lot of Jacobites to find a satisfactory sanctuary in Europe. In February 1748 he journeyed to Krakow on a mission to see whether he could fake his own death and live incognito in Poland, hoping to secure his son's inheritance back in Britain. The plan fell through, and he died in the Low Countries in 1760.

The Jacobite connection with Poland has come sharply back into focus in the twenty-first century through a remarkable book by Peter Pininski, *The Stuarts' Last Secret*. The main contention of this work is that the royal Stuart line did not die with either Charlotte, Duchess of Albany, nor with her son Charles, Count Roehenstart, but that the latter's sister also had children and descendants. Her name was Marie Victoire Roehenstart and she had a son in the early nineteenth century named Antime de Nikorowicz. Antime's own son Charles came to a bizarre end after he had a dispute with another man and participated in a so-called 'American duel'. This entailed drawing out one of two bullets concealed in a bag. Selecting a black bullet meant that the unlucky man who drew it would agree to commit suicide within the year. Antime honoured this bizarre Victorian contract. Exactly one year later he travelled to Versailles in France and shot himself dead at the end of August 1859. He was 28 years old. His son, another Antime, died in 1908 and left only daughters to succeed him. Peter Pininski claims descent from the female line; his ancestress being Marie Victoire's granddaughter Julia. Much of his book consists of a highly detailed account of his family in Poland and elsewhere up to the present date. However, some scholars have taken issue with some of the family connections detailed in the work.

The melancholy history of the royal Stuart family includes diversions that hold some fascination for latter-day Jacobites and 'legitimists' who tenaciously trace the labyrinthine descendants of the dynasty through the strange, winding paths of aristocratic European genealogy. For these adherents to the house of Stuart it is a matter of significance that there is an alternative, Jacobite and Stuart succession to the throne of Great Britain, even if the matter has little historical significance and there was no possibility that any member of this bloodline would ever attain the crown. The princely houses that inherited the right to Jacobite succession seemed at best disinterested, and sometimes embarrassed, by this aspect of their birthright.

Following the death of Cardinal Henry Stuart in 1808, the ghostly royalist Jacobite torch passed to King Charles Emmanuel IV of Sardinia, who was a descendant of Princess Henrietta, a daughter of Charles I who married Philip, Duke of Orleans. The succession continued through the dukes of Modena and was inherited through marriage by a royal family in Bavaria. The current holder of the succession is Franz, Duke of Bavaria. None of those who fell into this alternative, Jacobite birthright claimed the throne of Great Britain, nor were interested overly in this part of their heritage. The dynastic Jacobite succession was just an incidental appendance carried around with a portmanteau of other hereditary titles by several families far removed from the British kingdom.

Chapter 16

The Last Pretender

A century after the Sobieskis had left the scene, another supposed Stuart prince came to Scotland and began to promote himself as the Jacobite messiah. Despite a very minor flurry of publicity, most of the population was curiously muted about his claims. The unlikely self-proclaimed lost prince was a Belgian national named Michael Lafosse, who awarded himself the name HRH Prince Michael James Alexander Stewart, 7th Count of Albany, and claimed that he was the product of a royal bloodline through his mother, descendant of a secret marriage of Charles Edward Stuart, a union that no reputable historian believes. The newly discovered prince raised a few supporters in Scotland and even published a fulsome book about his pedigree and claims that rose to number two in the bestseller lists in that country. It was as if the Sobieski brothers had been reborn.

Much like the Sobieskis, Lafosse claimed to have documentary evidence to support his ancestry when he settled in Scotland in 1976 at the age of 18. He stated that Prince Charles Edward Stuart had received papal dispensation to dissolve his marriage to Princess Louise of Stolberg-Gedern in 1784 and the following year married Marguerite Marie Therese O'Dea d'Audibert de Lussan, the Countess de Massillan, soon producing an heir. No reputable historian believes there was such a marriage. The Lafosse legend states that the boy, Edward, was given the full birth name Edouard Jacques Stuardo, later known as Count Stuarton. The story elaborates that the Hanoverian establishment connived with Cardinal Henry, Duke of York, to expunge all knowledge of his brother's son and heir from history.

The secret son of the Young Pretender was raised in Sardinia and died in 1845 and was succeeded by his son, Prince Henry Edward Benedict (d. 1869), whose son Prince Charles Benedict James died in 1887, possibly murdered by British agents. Prince Michael the Belgian was allegedly descended from this shadowy offshoot of the Stuarts. His genealogical claim was oddly disjointed in various aspects, not least the absolute absence of any real supporting evidence to support his dynastic assertions. Michael wished to be accepted as King Alexander IV of Scotland; not of England, since his family had graciously dropped their claim to rule that nation in 1913. His idea was that he should be the progressive head of an independent socialist Scotland.

The documents he claimed to have included a birth certificate that authenticated his identity as Prince Michael James Stewart, 7th Count of Albany, and a letter from a senior Vatican official regarding the secret second marriage of Prince Charles Edward. After his arrival in his Scotland, Prince Michael went to work in a tartan gift shop and started to publicise his royalist claims. Although most people who noticed regarded the would-be prince with bemused indifference or embarrassment, he fitted in well with an eccentric aspect of genteel Edinburgh. Also living in the city during his time was an elderly English lady who had once been a playwright and who was convinced that she was the reincarnation of King James IV of Scotland.

Lafosse worked to build a profile in Scottish nationalist circles over several years, appearing at meetings and commemorations of historical events, an infiltration made by aligning his royal rights with an overt sympathy with Scottish demands for self-determination. Some of those he courted should definitely have known better but were still enveloped by the fairytale. Lafosse's claims were too extraordinary to attract the main body of Scottish nationalism, though he did appear at fringe meetings, such as a meeting of the Scottish Patriots Group in June 1979. Present at this meeting were members of the militant Sìol nan Gàidheal movement and the eminent senior nationalist Wendy Wood, who had taken a shine to the supposed prince.

To bolster his authority, Michael stated that in 1992 he was elected as head of the prestigious European Council of Princes, a constitutional advisory body affiliated with the European Parliament. It was claimed that this organisation was founded in 1946 by the influential nobleman Otto von Hapsburg, though this gentleman denied all knowledge of it.

One of the most prominent supporters of Prince Michael was Laurence Garner, an author who wrote extensively on the Grail, Knight Templars and the bloodline of Jesus Christ. He supported the idea that the blood of Jesus is represented in several European royal lines, not least the house of Stewart (Prince Michael's preferred spelling). Prince Michael himself subscribed to the shadowy beliefs of conspiratorial bloodlines, contributing to the introduction of a book that said that Princess Diana was assassinated partly because of her connection with this secret strand of royalty.

This part of Lafosse's claims run parallel with the even more opaque world of modern-day secret organisations who seem to have their fingers in every left-field mystical pie. One of the first leading lights to emerge from the Templar undergrowth in the 1950s was Pierre Plantard. He claimed that he was the representative of a royal bloodline, descended from the seventh-century French king Dagobert II. Gardner's *Bloodline of the Holy Grail* (for which Lafosse wrote the introduction) asserts that the blood of Christ has been consciously transmitted as a living relic through various royal lines in Europe, including of course the Scottish royal line represented by Lafosse. Although a monumental, grandiose and possibly blasphemous claim by the Belgian, the belief in this central notion, linking Christ to the grail and European royalty, was nothing new. The heady mix of messianic descent, the Holy Grail, plus Knights Templar conspiracy has been written about for decades. But there is no evidence that the original Jacobites subscribed to such ideas and nor did the neo-Jacobites at the tail end of the nineteenth century. One modern French pseudo-Jacobite organisation in France links the royal Stuarts with the ancient French king Charlemagne.

Doubts about Lafosse's claims came from many directions. Both the Court of the Lord Lyon in Edinburgh, which regulates Scottish titles, and Debrett's stated that they did not support his claim of royal descent. Researchers were able to pick apart the delicate claims of the Jacobite heir with relative ease. Martino Giusti, an official in the Vatican archive, denied having authored the letter regarding the annulment and remarriage of the Young Pretender. A statement from the registrar in Brussels declared that the royal had been born plain Michael Roger Lafosse. This was countered by Lafosse, who said this birth certificate was a forgery and part of a British conspiracy sponsored by the house of Windsor. In 1980 a report into the Lafosse claim was completed by Jack S. Macdonald. This followed an investigation by a group of prominent Scots, some of whom had met the young foreigner and liked him but had grown concerned about his claims. This group included Wendy Wood, the writer Nigel Tranter and A. J. Stewart, aka Ada F. Kay, the writer who claimed to be the reborn embodiment of King James IV. The eminent Glasgow lawyer James Docherty was one of those who voiced doubt about the Belgian's identity, along with Guy Stair Sainty. Macdonald's report concluded with the stark sentence: 'This report must therefore find that the claimant is a forger and a fraud.' Despite this, sadly, Wendy Wood did not believe the findings and supported Prince Michael until her death, at the age of 88, the following year.

As a side-line to his royalist and literary activities Lafosse began to sell knighthoods, damehoods and other titles in the Order of the Temple of Jerusalem, mostly to Americans. He also stood unsuccessfully as an MEP in the Czech Republic in 2004. When the genealogist and historian Anthony Adolph and Lafosse appeared on a BBC TV show by Ruby Wax in 2002, he was faced with the awkward position of having to say he did not believe in his claimed ancestry. The British authorities paid little heed to Michael Lafosse, probably on the basis that his claims were an irrelevance. The quietly spoken, bespectacled Belgian was devoid of any threatening firebrand quality that might have alarmed the establishment. As Clive Cheesman commented, Michael succeeded, albeit to a limited extent, by exploiting the 'growing contemporary lack of interest in the authority of monarchy, as opposed to its soap-opera aspects'.

By some oversight, Michael was granted naturalisation as a British subject in 2001 under the dubious name of Michael James Alexander Stewart of Albany. But in July 2006, following renewed revelations that his birth certificate had been forged, Michael Lafosse was obliged to return to his native Belgium. Belgian authorities revealed that Lafosse was the son of a shopworker, not Baron Lafosse as he claimed. Neither was his mother HRH Princess Renée Stewart, Lady Derneley, descendant of the royal house of Stuart, but plain Renée Julienne Dée, and Michael went back to live quietly with her, an exile from his supposed own people.

Lafosse was merely the latest generation of fake Jacobite royalty. The writer Compton Mackenzie wryly commented on the phenomenon and stated that in his time, there was a man living in the east of Scotland who alleged he was the direct heir of King James II and VII, and there was another man who claimed to be the heir of the Old Pretender by an early marriage.

Chapter 17

Outlanders and Others

The modern picture of the Jacobite in the popular mind is drawn from a number of sources that have mainly dealt with the rebellion of 1745 and its aftermath or concentrated on the adventurous career of Bonnie Prince Charlie. While there has inevitably been greater varieties of exploration of the different facets and periods of the movement in literature, there has also been coverage in both film and TV. The moving image has not been kind to Jacobitism and has thrown up some strange anomalies. In the 1940s movie audiences were presented with the peculiarity of David Niven as Bonnie Prince Charlie. Niven doubtless had the charisma to portray the character, but his obvious Englishness (despite sometimes claiming to have been born in Kirriemuir) detracted from the veracity of his portrayal. By far the greatest presence in film has been in versions of Robert Louis Stevenson's *Kidnapped*, which has notched up seven movie versions between 1917 and 1995, plus at least one television adaptation. Of the films, the majority were made entirely in America, including the 1960 version released by Walt Disney. Michael Caine's portrayal of Alan Breck Stuart in the reasonably decent 1971 film ranks with Niven in its oddness. Casting natives in key roles of Scottish Jacobite films has never been a prime consideration for filmmakers.

A third contender for culturally inappropriate Jacobite portrayal goes to Errol Flynn for his role in *The Master of Ballantrae* (1953). This film removes all the subtlety and complexity of R. L. Stevenson's fine novel and leaves a hollow husk of swashbuckling derring-do. Luckily such films are no longer produced. Returning to the source material, Stevenson's 1889 novel is one of his less well-known works, telling the story of a laird's family from south-west Scotland torn apart by competing loyalties to the government and Jacobite sides. The master of the title fights for the Stuart insurgents while his brother is a Whig who stays loyally at home. The book recalls Stevenson's own *The Strange Case of Dr Jekyll and Mr Hyde* from several years earlier, but pins down the malignant duality in human nature to a particularly Scottish context much like James Hogg's classic *The Private Memoirs and Confessions of a Justified Sinner*. Unlike the charming Alan Breck of *Kidnapped*, the Jacobite main character here, James Durisdeer, is a devilishly charismatic, almost demonic figure with few redeeming characteristics, subverting the prevailing Scottish preference for the Jacobite side. His restless travels after Culloden correspond with the lived experience of many Jacobite exiles, albeit the dramatic exaggeration of his journeying threatens to disturb the narrative.

In more recent times, the Scottish Jacobite experience has been explored in features such as *Chasing the Deer* (1994). The latter was one of a series of big-screen representations of historical Scotland, a small flurry of above-average films that included other titles such as *Rob Roy* (1995) and of course *Braveheart* (1995), plus others that tell the story of Robert the Bruce. Mainstream modern television has mainly shied away from any sustained examination of any part of the Jacobite history, despite the obvious appeal of the drama of the 1745 uprising and other events. One reason for the aversion to the subject must be its continuing intimate relationship with Scottish nationalism, independence and various forms of self-determination. The serious debate on this subject reignited in the 1970s and never quite went away, through the Thatcher years, the creation of the Scottish parliament and the referendum on Scottish independence. Documentary filmmakers have baulked at the idea of tackling the complexities and controversies of the subject apart from the stark docudrama approach of Peter Watkins' *Culloden* in 1964. The latter's resonance had further effect in the shadow of the Vietnam War.

The successful *Outlander* series of books started in the early 1990s and later generated an equally successful television series. The books were originated by the American author Diana Gabaldon and present a plausible Jacobite-era landscape that is arresting and appealing but sometimes struggles to play off its romantic elements against strict historical accuracy. A third element, the time travelling of its principal female character, is central to the series and possibly the least successful element. *Outlander*'s conformity to accuracy was confirmed in a rather backhanded way by the Scottish writer Deborah Dennison, who likens the depiction of Highland culture to the bigoted view disseminated by English society in the eighteenth century. Gabaldon pointed out that she has carefully conducted historical research but said that no one should take a television series based on time travel as being a factual representation of anything. Modern media representations of Scottish culture generated by non-Scots will always be divisive. For every person claiming that clan society was a perfect model of propriety that treated all its members fairly, there are others who accept that modern perceptions of the Jacobites and other aspects of their nation will inevitably be skewed. And for every *Outlander* impersonator who touts himself as a 'genuine' Highlander, there will be others in the long-deprived glens who simply accept the renewed attention the series has brought to the region, where the need for cultural integrity always sits beside economic imperative.

Epilogue

The Jacobite Hall of Mirrors

As the centuries have progressed, the meaning of Jacobitism has expanded and changed. Its main detractors, those British establishment figures from the Whig oligarchy who strongly supported the Hanoverian regime, could not even agree on the best derogatory names for the figureheads of the detested and supposedly vanquished Stuart regime. The name-calling started early, even before the hapless house of Stuart fled to the continent. To Nell Gwynne, mistress of King Charles II, the king's lugubrious brother the Duke of York (future King James II) was Dismal Jimmy. Still adored by many as the rightful king, some of the sheen was worn off his reputation by his woeful political and military defects. One Irish poet, dismissive of the king abandoning the country after defeat at the Battle of Boyne in 1691, memorably dubbed him *Seamas an Chaca*, James the Shit, surely his most derogatory appellation. Similar sentiments were expressed about his grandson, Prince Charles Edward, leaving the field at Culloden and leaving his mainly Scottish supporters to their own fate. He may not have been called an Italian coward at that pivotal moment, as legend has it, but doubts about his character grew from that day.

Horace Mann, a British official in Italy, kept a feverish eye on the exiled Stuart court and sought to minimise their significance with his caustic reporting. Among other epithets, he dubbed the son of James II the Old Phantom. Mr James Misfortune was another mocking put-down attached to the Old Pretender (sometimes changed to Old Mr Misfortune), emphasising his comedic irrelevance. In his younger days in France, the swarthy and solemn nationless king had been known to some as the Blackbird.

Charles Edward Stuart (Carluccio to his fond father) had a similar array of bynames: he was variously the Italian, the Young Pretender, the Mock Prince and the Young Chevalier. He used the nom de guerre Chevalier de George while observing the Spanish campaign in Italy as an adolescent. Jacobite supporters had their own secondary names for their kings and princes. Romantically, the exiled Stuart royals were Kings Over the Water. Idolising Scottish Gaels called the hero of the '45 Teàrlach, which mutated into the English Charlie. Out of necessity (for there was always an English price on his head), Charles adopted pseudonyms of his own to throw the bloodhounds off his trail. Following Culloden and temporarily in the guise of a woman, he famously became Betty Bourke, a most unbecoming maid. Towards the end of his life, when the hoped-for crown appeared forlorn, he took the cognomen Count d'Albany. The variety of names Charles Edward adopted may also say something about his inner struggle for identity. At various times he was known as Mr Douglas, Bidolphe, William Bidle, even the Wildman. More historically fitting was the epithet bestowed upon him in a letter by a Northumberland Jacobite to a similarly circumspect friend in 1750. He referred to the exiled royal as the 'young Goodman of Bellnaigh', a reference to the incognito of King James V of Scotland who used to tramp the countryside in disguise for the sake of adventure and to gauge the true condition of the nation. Similarly, his father earned the sardonic epithet Jamie the Rover in recognition of his exiled court shifting from France to Italy. To identify him out loud was a risk for supporters and enemies could not bear to utter his true name. Like the Evil One, he had to be called something else; so, to some in Britain he was spoken of as the Rash Adventurer. Such a variety of aliases, albeit none of them fond, appears oddly empowering to the Pretenders and their nearest and dearest. After all, why go to the trouble of inventing nicknames for individuals who are believed to be utterly irrelevant? The prince was of course many things to many people: prince, fraud, leader, romantic ideal, but also a drunk and woman beater.

Where does the spirit of Jacobitism lie in the modern age and what does it mean? Many have tried to distil its essence while many others have sought to exorcise what they perceive as its sickly image, a historical pollutant particular to modern Scotland. The undying figure of Bonnie Prince Charlie survived all the best efforts to banish him to the netherworld. He manifests in strange ways. The Scottish author Violet Tweedale relates a story about a visit to the Highland home of Sybil Blunt-Mackenzie, Countess of Cromartie. Sybil, a gifted friend of W. B. Yeats, was renowned for her spiritual gifts and strange things often happened in her presence. On this occasion, the guests in her house included Prince Arthur of Connaught, a grandson of Queen Victoria, who happened to comment on a framed letter on the wall that he identified as being written by the 'Pretender'. The Scottish guests present were appalled by the word, coming as it did from a Hanoverian royal. Tweedale corrected him by saying that they always referred to the writer as Prince Charles Edward Stuart. To please all parties, Prince Arthur laughed and said, 'I beg his pardon and all yours.' The Scots present were appeased. But that was not the end of the matter.

Sybil later came to Violet's room and announced that she had just seen the spirit of Charles Edward Stuart. He stood looking at her from the far end of the room, smiling, then slowly crossed the room and vanished through the wall. Tweedale theorised that the guests had created a thought form earlier in the evening when Prince Arthur had made his blunder and their collective emotion had summoned the shade of the prince from the astral plane, or perhaps from the evocative Scottish ether. No further sighting occurred, but the author put the experience in context:

> I doubt if it is possible for an English person to comprehend what it means to be a Jacobite. One is born a Jacobite or one is not. I was born a Jacobite and I never lose my passionate love and regret for the sufferings and sorrows of Prince Charles Edward…What was the power in you…that drew from countless women and men that unswerving devotion?

(In true contrarian style, Bonnie Prince Charlie is also said to haunt the manor of Westbrook Place, Godalming, Surrey, which he fleetingly visited incognito.)

It might be said that, even in life, Charles Edward Stuart became a thought form, a living ghost, in the long years after Culloden. There is a poignant comparison to be made between this living death and another, impersonal fate suffered by the place where he had his greatest adventure. The Highlands, the cultural region called the *Gaeltacht*, had a tortuous, lingering decline after the Jacobite defeat. Scotland mourned Charles, its own independence and sense of identity, and something else indefinable, all bound up together. This intertwined or correlated fate is perfectly pictured by Iain Chrichton Smith in his poem 'Prince Charles', where the adventurous royal retreats from Scotland, to the fresh land he hoped to put his marks on, and retreats to drink in the lush pastures of Italy. Scotland is left desolate in the wake of his failed adventure.

Might-have-beens or wishful thinking history have been a component of Celtic thinking since the Middle Ages. The frustration of loss in war, being the perpetual underdog, having to accept defeat at the hands of a wanton English nation, has not been easy for a small portion of these nations' imaginative lights. Some in the Celtic north and west looked to what might have been otherwise. What, for example, if Culloden had not been lost, if the Jacobites had actually won? From a Scottish perspective, Compton Mackenzie considered this:

> The American colonies would never have been lost. The French Revolution might never have happened...The long martyrdom of Ireland would have been averted. The decline of Scotland into a provincial appendage would have been avoided. Religious toleration would have been achieved long before it was. There might have been no exploitation of the poor by cynical industrialisation.

Some of this may be true; most is not. The idea that the Young Pretender, had he become King Charles III in real life, would have abolished the Act of Union between Scotland and England is far from certain. At times he did give lip service to this cherished ideal of many Scots, but leaders have a habit of forgetting pledges when they take on the mantle of power. The allure of the Young Pretender captured Mackenzie as it has done others. To him, the Jacobite movement was an emotional, cultural and symbolic totem. W. B. Yeats also played with this idealised symbolism of the Jacobites. Best remembered today for being the author of *Whisky Galore*, but this was only one production in a wide-ranging career that involved not only literature but soldiering and spying. Despite being English born, he took a keen interest in his family's homeland in Scotland and lived there for long periods and wrote several books on Prince Charles Edward Stuart. Among his Jacobite mementoes was a single hair from the prince's head that he kept in a gold locket and a small Sacred Heart amulet worn by Macdonald of Keppoch at Culloden. He was also actively involved in early neo-Jacobite movements. He became a member of the Thames Valley Legitimist League, the Society of the White Carnation and the White Rose Association. He later became a governor-general of the Royal Stuart Society and a co-founder of the National Party of Scotland, one of the forerunners of the Scottish National Party.

The Jacobites, to him, embodied a spirit of purity, in the same way he envisaged the Reformation as a victory for barbarism and allied in his mind with Communism and Nazi-ism. Jacobites in their heyday may have imagined that they were a political and spiritual vanguard far superior than their ideological opponents, but this dangerous imprinting of the past with black and white concepts of morality can be tricky. Some early Scottish Jacobites took even earlier delight in persecuting Covenanters in the seventeenth century, who themselves thought they were God's own chosen tribe. History is littered with movements who believe they are eternally wronged martyrs punished by being displaced by more degenerate ideologies.

Jacobitism continues to play various tricks with the mind. While perhaps a sober Whiggish writer can dismiss the whole history of it as a starry-eyed nonsense, for others it can be a different matter. Scottish people have complex attitudes to the Jacobites. The poet Hugh MacDiarmid used the figure of Charles Edward Stuart and the Jacobites to express contrary emotions about the past and different facets of Scottish consciousness. In one poem he caustically noted that those modern Scots who waxed sentimental over the Jacobites were mostly reactionary types who would have run a mile if they had been alive at the time of the '45 and confronted by a bona fide Jacobite. In another poem, he reminds readers of the fatal glamour of the prince: 'a' isna gowd that glitters', and Charles Edward is likened to a perilous living flame that enchants the minds and hearts of those who would be better off showing their devotion to Scotland. Still, the '45 and all its connotations was a deeply significant and symbolic event to MacDiarmid and others in the twentieth-century Scottish Renaissance.

MacDiarmid's quote about the lost prince at the start of this book expressed the wry belief that those Scots who sentimentally wished the prince over the water would one day return would have been horrified, and indeed against him, had he magically reappeared and scuttled the status quo. Though the '45 rebellion itself, in retrospect, was a highly symbolic as well as a historic event to the poet, the actual prince was a divisive figure.

In Ireland, Jacobitism sank like a shadow in the bog. Most latter-day Irish nationalists happily shrugged off the colonial sham of loyalty to the Stuart dynasty, though others adopted a more nuanced opinion. W. B. Yeats saw the defeat of this ruling house as the end of true nobility and artistry and the connection with the profound, mystical past of native culture in Ireland: 'the Battle of the Boyne…overwhelmed a civilisation full and religion and myth and brought in its place unintelligible laws planned out upon a great blackboard'. For all that, Yeats was no neo-Jacobite; it was just one more historical, spiritual and symbolic element in his belief system. His flirtation with Jacobitism, slight as it was, probably jarred with many of his countrymen. Many other Irish, who wanted to be free of the taint of Britishness, came to regard the Stuarts as an irrelevance and the Williamite War between James II and his usurper was merely a struggle between two equally foreign powers that unfortunately took place in their land. Some in Scotland may have viewed the disastrous uprisings of 1715 and 1745 fought mainly in their country as having even more detrimental results for their nation, for the sake of the ambitions of a debased, now alien monarchy.

Popular sentiment linking Jacobite feeling with a hatred of British rule had lingered among the Irish population a little beyond the mid-eighteenth century. In late 1759, a riot among the 'lower orders' in Dublin was prompted by a public address of loyalty to King George. By the end of the eighteenth century many in Ireland had discarded the old, wrong-headed attachment to Jacobitism. In the 1790s the Irish republican Wolfe Tone dismissed a fanciful French suggestion to implant the Stuart dynasty in Ireland. He scornfully rejected any 'Henrician restoration', a reference to the Young Pretender's brother Henry, Cardinal Duke of York. The twentieth-century nationalist James Connolly again dismissed the Stuarts, damning James II as 'the most worthless representative of a worthless race that ever sat on a throne'. Historians in Ireland have been overwhelmingly damning of the once very apparent Irish Jacobite attachment.

But there will always be exceptions to the prevailing ideas that historians and nationalists have about their national past. James Lees-Milne reports that, as late as 1901, a handkerchief soaked with the blood of Cardinal Henry Stuart, Duke of York, was believed by some in Ireland to be a relic that had the power to cure scrofula. The same aura of holiness was believed about the Stuarts by those more intellectual modern Jacobites who venerated the royal house for its supposed sacrificial and semi-divine associations. In their elevated opinion, King Charles I was of course a martyr, and even his fairly worldly ancestress Mary, Queen of Scots, was a candidate for sainthood because of her obstinate attachment to Catholicism rather than common sense. Obstinacy in religious matter might be one of the true hallmarks of the royal Stuarts. The small but persistent modern cult that venerated them had little time for politics, but ardently marked out the calendar in ritually significant dates that marked the martyrdom of those kings and queen and other important anniversaries.

In Ireland too, more subtle traces of Jacobite heritage lingered among the participants of the 1916 uprising. Some of the signatories of the nationalist proclamation that year were involved in the translation of Irish Jacobite poetry, and the anthem of the Irish volunteers, 'Óró 'sé do bheatha abhaile', was an old Jacobite rebel tune disguised and reworked as a modern Irish republican battle cry.

In the modern age, some people are attracted to the story of the Jacobites because it represents a variation on an attachment to those worthy movements in history that seem attractive because they were doomed to failure. Here the Jacobites jostle for attention on the doomed history shelf alongside the Confederates, Knights Templars, the Cathars, Covenanters, and many other dispossessed, dusty movements. Some of those attracted to the doleful cult of the Stuarts may believe that the whole long line of Scottish and British monarchs was ill-fated even before the curse of the Covenanters was placed upon them in the late seventeenth century. Such a view persisted, even among professional historians. In a capricious aside when writing about the birth of Prince Charles Edward Stuart, Alexander Ewald wondered, 'Were it not better for the God-cursed dynasty to die out and cease provoking the Divine wrath?' Judgement from deity aside, it could be argued that it was a mercy that the direct line of the royal Stuarts did indeed die out; otherwise, their hapless descendants would have been doomed to live marooned in the shadowlands occupied by other ex-royals in Europe.

Modern historians who represent a continuum of the old Whig view of British history are apt to view the Jacobites as an anomaly or an irrelevance. From the beginning of the eighteenth century jubilant supporters of the new British reign were asserting that the old Stuarts were merely 'an Italianized relic of an outdated form of sovereignty' (as one modern reviewer put it). Some recent historians have tried to rebalance the view of the Jacobites, but there has been resistance to change. In 1986, the academic David Cannadine railed against 'the new Jacobite view of history, a wilfully perverse celebration of such obscurantist troglodytes as the Young Pretender'. Such dismissive views, often wrapped in a condescending cover of humour, are all too common. Even more recently, Christopher Duffy asked an assortment of professional historians what they thought about the Jacobite forces during the '45. Their answers were a variation on the glib description of 'thieving Catholic Highland bastards'. There may be some humour in the woefully misjudged and doomed efforts of the Jacobites to achieve the Stuart restoration, but measured against the suffering of those involved, it is a darkly patterned humour, a plaid woven in black and blood red. At one level, the struggle between dynasties in the century between 1688 and 1788 is almost comical. What was there to choose between the Hanoverians – uncouth, Teutonic and unpleasant – pitted against the latter Stuarts – Papist, doom ridden and alien?

Still, the many-sided thought-form of Prince Charles Edward Stuart ensured that he lived in the popular imagination far longer than the more worthy men and women who followed him. He remains the last Jacobite, still alive by virtue of a legend that is more complex and intriguing than the actual man. Stripped of the suffocating layers of romance, the attempt by Charles Edward to recover his father's throne was a remarkable act of sustained bravery, albeit ultimately a failure. His personal characteristics of fortitude and bravery as he eluded government troops in the wilds of Scotland stand in stark contrast with his later dissolute behaviour. Although the 'Bonnie Prince' legend kept people spellbound for generations, what is possibly more intriguing in the legendary perception of the prince is his shadow personality as a fugitive, man in disguise and almost trickster figure. Incognito, he became an alarming master of disguise: a Catholic, Stuart, Masonic, non-English bugbear. Now of course, his escapades to trick his enemy seem rather quaint: dressing up as an Irish maid in the Hebrides or painting his face red and adopting thick black eyebrows in Rome. But he worried his enemies, to some extent, until his death.

He eluded the Hanoverians for so long in Britain and abroad that he became a kind of bogeyman that haunted their imaginations. The Young Pretender was everywhere and nowhere, evading the keen eyes of British spies, and even having the audacity (according to one tale) to show up incognito at the wedding of King George III to Charlotte Sophia of Mecklenburg-Strelitz in London in 1761. There had been rumours of this royal Jack-in-the-Box appearing in London several times in the early 1750s, but the stories were fabricated by scandal-hungry gossips.

The unsettling transformation from a fearless prince regent leading an uprising to a violent dipsomaniac seemed to confound a host of observers, both contemporary and later. How could such a thing have happened? The former prime minister Archibald Primrose, Earl of Roseberry, wrote of his tripartite life and afterlife: 'He disappears [after defeat] for a decade and emerges a changed man: bloated, drunken, half-imbecile, half brute, and so he ends his life. Then again, by a magic unconscious touch of History, he is transmuted for ever into a paladin…' The Jacobite spectre was laid, at least temporarily, by Hanoverian indifference. When King George II was told the story that the Pretender was in London and boldly asked what he would do about it, he merely shrugged and replied, 'I shall do nothing. When he is tired of England, he will go abroad again.' German George had learned English insouciance and grasped the true irrelevance of his family's hereditary enemy. While the Stuarts represented to some the only legitimate royal family of Great Britain, the Hanoverians were a cynical imposition artificially elevated onto the apex of society by a Whig regime that had hijacked power for its own interests. There was nothing saintly, special or magical about the new German royals. It was only after they had bedded into their Britishness in the nineteenth century that they felt able to assume the ancient prerogatives of regality, and only then by sleight of hand. Queen Victoria slyly became the embodiment of Britishness by consciously assuming the discarded mantle of royalty that her Stuart forbears had so carelessly dropped.

Bibliography

A. M., 'Cluny Macpherson at Cluny Castle', *The Celtic Magazine* 30 April 1878, Vol. 3, 201–8.

Adams, Ian. *Cargoes of Despair and Hope: Scottish Emigration to North America, 1603–1803*, Edinburgh, 1993.

Adolph, Anthony. *Tracing Your Scottish Ancestry*, London, 2008.

Amulree, Lord. 'Dr Archibald Cameron', *Medical History* 15.3 July 1971, 23–40.

Anderson, R. C. 'British and American Officers in the Russian Navy'. *The Mariner's Mirror* 33:1, 1941, 17–27.

Anonymous. *A Candid and Impartial Account of the Behaviour of Simon, Lord Lovat*, London, 1747.

Anonymous. *The Young Pretender's Destiny Unfolded: Being an Exact Account of Several Prodigies Seen in the Highlands*, London, 1745.

Askwith, Richard. 'The Man Who Would Be King'. *The Guardian*, 24 March 1999.

Baigent, Michael & Leigh, Richard. *The Temple and the Lodge*, New York, 2011.

Boswell, James. *Boswell's Journal of a Tour to the Hebrides with Samuel Johnson*, London, 1936.

Brock, William Ranulf. *Scotus Americanus: A Survey of the Sources for Links between Scotland and America in the Eighteenth Century*, Edinburgh, 1982.

Bruce, Maurice. 'Jacobite Relations with Peter the Great', *The Slavonic and East European Review* 14, No. 41, January 1936, 343–362.

Buchanan, Craig. 'The Sobieski Stuart Compositions', *Notes and Queries* 61, Issue 4, 2014, 531–536.

Bueltmann, Tanja, Hinson, Andrew & Morton, Graeme. *The Scottish Diaspora*, Edinburgh, 2013.

Burton, John Hill. *The Scot Abroad*, new edition, Edinburgh, 1881.

Cameron, John. 'A Song to Dr Cameron', www.lochiel.net/archives/arch077.html

Camp, Anthony J. 'New Light on The Sobieski Stuarts', https://anthonyjcamp.com/pages/anthony-j-camp-sobieski-stuarts

Campbell, Lord Archibald. *Records of Argyll, Legends, Traditions, and Recollections of Argyllshire Highlanders*, Edinburgh, 1885.

Carney, Seamus. *The Appin Murder, the Killing of the Red Fox*, 1989, reprinted Edinburgh, 1994.

Cheesman, Clive. *Rebels, Pretenders and Imposters*, New York, 2000.

Churton, Tobias. *Aleister Crowley, the Biography*, London, 2011.

Churton, Tobias. *The Invisible History of the Rosicucians, the World's Most Mysterious Secret Society*, Rochester, 2009.

Coleman, James. *Remembering the Past in Nineteenth-Century Scotland: Commemoration, Nationality and Memory*, Edinburgh, 2014.

Coleman, Keith. 'Jacobite Characters, Part Two', Angus Folklore Blogspot, http://angusfolklore.blogspot.com/search?q=balnamoon

Corp, Edward. 'Stuart and Stuardo: James III and his Neopolitan Cousin', *Papers of the British School at Rome* 83, 2015, 221–243.

Crichton Smith, Ian. *The Exiles*, Manchester, 1984.

Cunningham, Callum. '"Rebels Without a Cause": The External Jacobite Diasporas, 1688–1788', *SATH History Teaching Review Yearbook* 27, 2020, 4–17.

D'Arlincourt, Viscount. *The Three Kingdoms: England, Scotland, Ireland*, Volume 2, London, 1844.

Dennison, Deborah. 'Outlander promotes a deeply distorted view of Gaelic life and culture', *The Scotsman*, 29 January 2023.

Devine, Thomas M. *The Scottish Clearances: A History of the Dispossessed, 1600–1900*, London, 2018.

Dewar, John. 'The Appin Murders', *The Penguin Book of Scottish Folktales*, Neil Philip ed., London, 1995, 255–279.

Dobson, David. *Scottish Emigration to Colonial America, 1607–1785*, Georgia, 1994, reprinted 2004.

Douglas, Hugh. *Bonnie Prince Charlie in Love*, Stroud, 2002.

Douglas, Hugh. *Jacobite Spy Wars, Moles, Rogues and Treachery*, Stroud, 1999.

Downer, Martyn. 'The Englishman who saved the Jacobites' Gold,' *Spink Insider*, 9 April 2020, https://insider.spink.com/2020/04/09/the-englishman-who-saved-the-jacobites-gold/

Duffy, Christopher. *The '45, Bonnie Prince Charlie and the Untold Story of the Jacobite Rising*, London, 2003.

Duncombe-Jewell, Louis Charles Richard. 'The True Jacobitism, A Survival', *The Albemarle* 2, No. 1, July 1892, 31–34.

Ewald, Alexander Charles. *The Life and Times of Prince Charles Stuart, Count of Albany*, 2 volumes, London, 1875.

Fletcher, Ian. *W. B. Yeats and His Contemporaries*, New York, 1987.

Forbes, Archibald. 'Real Stuarts or Bogus Stuarts', *New Review* 8, Issue 44, 1895, 73–84.

Forbes, Rev. Robert. *The Lyon in Winter*, 3 volumes, Edinburgh, 1895.

Forsyth, Rev. William. *In the Shadow of Cairngorm, Chronicles of the Unites Parishes of Abernethy and Kincardine*, Inverness, 1900.

Fox, E. T. 'Jacobitism and the "golden age" of piracy, 1715–1725', *International Journal of Maritime History* 22, No. 2, December 2010, 277–303.

Fraser, Duncan. *Glen of the Rowan Trees*, Montrose, 1973.

Galloway, Colin H. '"Have the Scotch no Claim upon the Cherokee?" Scots, Indians and Scots Indians in the American South', in *Global Migrations, The Scottish Diaspora Since 1600*, ed. Angela McCarthy & John M. McKenzie, Edinburgh, 2016, 81–97.

Gardner, Laurence. *Bloodline of the Holy Grail, the Hidden Lineage of Jesus Revealed*, Shaftesbury, 1996, reprinted 1997.

Gibson, Mary E. 'Dr Archibald Cameron (1707–1753)', *Journal of Medical Biography* 13, Issue 2, May 2005, 117–118.

Gordon, Seton. *Highways and Byways in the Central Highlands*, 1935, reprinted Edinburgh, 1995.

Grant, Elizabeth. *Memoirs of a Highland Lady, the Autobiography of Elizabeth Grant of Rothiemurchus,1797–1830*, Lady Strachey ed., London, 1911.

Gray, Affleck. *Legends of the Cairngorms*, Edinburgh, 1987.

Hamilton, Marion. 'The Loch ArkaigTreasure', *Miscellany of the Scottish History Society* 7, Edinburgh, 1941, 131–168.

Henderson, Jan-Andrew. *The Emperor's New Kilt, Two Secret Histories of Scotland*, Edinburgh, 2000.

Hesse, David. 'Re-enacting Scottish history in Europe', *Mysticism, Myth and Celtic Identity*, Marion Gibson, Shelley Trower & Garry Tregidda eds., London, 2013, 171–186.

Jardine, Jerry. 'The Stuart Pretenders', *Scottish Journal*, May 1999, republished, www.electricscotland.com/history/other/claimants_stewarts.htm

Jennings, I. J. ed. *The Croker Papers, the Correspondence and Diaries of the Late Right Honourable John William Croker*, Volume 1, 2nd Edition, London, 1885.

Johnsen, Aarne Odd. 'Jacobite Officers at Bergen, after the Battle of Culloden: Letters from the French Consul-General in Bergen', *The Scottish Historical Review* 57, No. 164, Part 2, October 1978, 186–196.

Jordan, Don & Walsh, Michael. *White Cargo, The Forgotten History of Britain's White Slaves in America*, Edinburgh, 2007.

Kidd, Colin. 'The Rehabilitation of Scottish Jacobitism,' *The Scottish Historical Review* 77, No. 203, Part 1, April 1998, 58–76.

Kopelev, D. N. '"Pirates Will More Pleasantly Accept the Patronage of His Imperial Majesty": Colonial Projects of Peter the Great and Jacobite Conspiracies (1718–1725)'. *Herald of the Russian Academy of Sciences* 92, Suppl. 8, 2022, S703–S712.

Lang, Andrew. 'The Mystery of James de La Cloche', *The Valet's Tragedy and Other Studies*, London, 1903, 228–257.

Lang, Andrew. *The Companions of Pickle*, London, 1898.

Lees-Milne, James. *The Last Stuarts: British Royalty in Exile*, London, 1983.

Lewis, Harry M. 'A "Project Was Contrived and Carryed On With Great Secrecy" 1: International Irish Jacobite Networks and the Madagascar Project, 1718–1723', *Northern Studies* 52, 2021, 137–163.

Lewis, Harry M. 'George Camocke's 1718 Proposal of a Jacobite–Pirate Alliance', *The Mariner's Mirror* 107:3, 2021, 366–370.

Love, Dane. *Jacobite Stories*, Glasgow, 2007.

Lowson, Alexander ed. *Caledonia, A Monthly Magazine of Literature, Antiquity, and Tradition, Mostly Northern*, Aberdeen,1895, 55–76.

MacDiarmid, Hugh. *The Complete Poems of Hugh MacDiarmid*, Michael Grieve & W. R. Aitken eds., revised edition, Harmondsworth, 1985.

Macdonald, Jack S. *Report Regarding Evidence of the Claim of Michael James Stewart or Michael Roger Lafosse*, 1 June 1980, https://priory-of-sion.com/posd/lafosse/lafosse.html

Macinnes, Alan. 'The Appin Murder: Jacobite Assassins or Campbell Killer', *Transactions of the Gaelic Society of Inverness* 78, 2015–2017, 324–348.

Mackenzie, Compton. *My Life and Times, 1891–1900*, London, 1963.

Mackenzie, Compton. *Prince Charlie and His Ladies*, New York, 1935.

Mackenzie, Nadine. *Darn Good Dandies!* Calgary, 2015.

MacKenzie, Niall. 'The Jacobites' "general": Spanish John's evidence for the history of military bagpiping', *Scottish Tradition* 25, 2000, 4–25.

Maclennan, Farquhar Stuart. *Early Scottish Influence in North America*, Montreal, 1898.

MacLeod, Rev. Walter. *A List of Persons Concerned in the Rebellion*, Scottish History Society, Volume 8, Edinburgh, 1890.

McFerran, Noel S. 'Prince Michael of Albany', *The Jacobite Heritage*, www.jacobite.ca/essays/lafosse.htm

McKenzie, Compton. *Prince Charlie*, London, 1932.

McLaren, Moray. *Bonnie Prince Charlie*, London, 1972.

Morgan Gwenda & Rushton, Peter. *Banishment in the Early Atlantic World: Convicts, Rebels and Slaves*, London, 2013.

Morrisby, Ted. *Unpackaged Tours: World Travels Off the Beaten Track*, New York, 1988.

Mullen, Stephen. 'The myth of Scottish slaves', Sceptical Scot, https://sceptical.scot/2016/03/the-myth-of-scottish-slaves/2016

Murdoch, Steve. 'Tilting at Windmills: The Order del Toboso as a Jacobite Social Network', *Loyalty and Identity Jacobites at Home and Abroad*, Paul Monod, Murray Pittock & Daniel Szechi eds., Basingstoke, 243–264.

Murdoch, Steve. *Network North, Scottish Kin, Commercial and Covert Associations in Northern Europe, 1603–1746*, Leiden, 2006.

Murphy, Seán. 'Irish Jacobitism and Freemasonry', *Eighteenth-Century Ireland / Iris an dá chultúr* 9, 1994, 75–82.

Ó Ciardha, Éamonn. *Ireland and the Jacobite Cause, 1685–1766*, Dublin, 2004.

Ó hÓgáin, Dáithí. *The Hero in Irish Folk History*, Gill & Macmillan Ltd., Dublin, 1985.

O' Keefe, Paul. *Culloden, Battle and Aftermath*, London, 2021.

Oates, Jonathan. *Sweet William or the Butcher: The Duke of Cumberland and the '45*, Halifax, 2008.

Owens, Peter. 'The legend of the princess in exile', *Otago Daily Times*, 16 August 2008.

Petrie, Charles. 'The Elibank Plot, 1752–3', *Transactions of the Royal Historical Society* 14, 1931, 175–196.

Picknett, Lynn & Prince, Clive. *The Sion Revelation: Inside the Shadowy World of Europe's Secret Masters*, London, 2006.

Pininski, Peter. *The Stuarts' Last Secret, The Missing Heirs of Bonnie Prince Charlie*, East Linton, 2002.

Pittock, Murray. *The Invention of Scotland: the Stuart Myth and the Scottish Identity, 1638 to Present*, London, 1991.

Prebble, John. *The King's Jaunt: George IV in Scotland, August 1822*, London, 1988.

Redman, Alvin. *The House of Hanover*, London, 1960.

Reid, A. G. 'The Wanderings of Strowan Robertson after Culloden', *Notes and Queries* 9, Issue 218, 1896, 161–162.

Ross, Peter. *Daunderlust*, Dingwall, 2014.

Schuchard, Marsha Keith. 'Lord George Gordon and Cabalistic Freemasonry: beating Jacobite swords into plough shares', *Secret Conversions to Judaism in Early Modern Europe*, Martin Muslow & Richard H. Popkin eds., Leiden, 2004, 183–232.

Schuchard, Marsha Keith. *Emanuel Swedenborg, Secret Agent on Earth and in Heaven*, Leiden, 2011.

Schuchard, Marsha Keith. *Jacobites, Jews, and Freemasons in Early Modern Sweden*, Leiden, 2012.

Scott, Walter. *Rob Roy*, Edinburgh, 1818.

Seward, Desmond. *The King Over the Water, A Complete History of the Jacobites*, Edinburgh, 2019.

Shaw, Michael. *The Fin-de-Siècle Scottish Revival: Romance, Decadence and Celtic Identity*, Edinburgh, 2019.

Sherburn, George. *Roehenstart, A Late Stuart Pretender*, Chicago, 1960.

Shield, Alice. *Henry Stuart, Cardinal of York and His Times*, London, 1908.

Steuart, A. Francis. *Scottish Influences in Russian History from the End of the 16th Century to the Beginning of the 19th Century*, Glasgow, 1913.

Stewart, Major General David. *Sketches of the Character, Manners, and Present State of the Highlanders of Scotland*, 3rd edition, Volume 1, Edinburgh, 1825.

Sutherland, Elizabeth. *Ravens and Black Rain, The Story of Highland Second Sight*, London, 1987.

Szechi, Daniel. *The Jacobites, Britain and Europe, 1699–1788*, 2nd edition, Manchester, 2019.

Tarantino, Giovanni. 'Jacques de la Cloche: A Stuart Pretender in the Seventeenth Century', *Archivum Historicum Societatis Iesu* 73, June–December 2004, 434–441.

Tayler, Alistair & Henrietta. *A Jacobite Exile*, London, 1937.

Tayler, Henrietta. 'Documents Relating to Prince Charles Edward's Grandson', *Miscellany of the Scottish History Society*, Volume 8, 1951, 117–135.

Thomson, George Malcolm. *A Kind of Justice, Two Studies in Treason*, London, 1970.

Thomson, James. *Recollections of A Speyside Parish*, Elgin, 1902.

Trevor-Roper, Hugh. *The Invention of Scotland, Myth and History*, New Haven, 2008.

Tweedale, Violet. *Ghosts I Have Seen, and Other Psychic Adventures*, New York, 1919.

Vaughan, Herbert M. *The Last of the Stuarts, Henry Stuart, Cardinal of York*, 2nd edition, New York, 1906.

Victoria, Queen. *More Leaves from the Journal of a Life in the Highlands*, 5th edition, London, 1884.

Washington, S. H. Lee. 'The Count of Roehenstart', Part 2, *Notes and Queries*, 198, June 1953, 244–248.

Waters, B. 'New Kings on Old Thrones', *Pearson's Magazine*, 5 February 1898.

Webb, James. *The Occult Underground*, La Salle, 1974.

Wemyss, David (Lord Elcho). *A Short Account of the Affairs of Scotland in the Years 1744, 1756, 1746*, Evan Charteris ed., Edinburgh, 1907.

Zimmermann, Doron. *The Jacobite Movement in Scotland and in Exile, 1746–1759*, Basingstoke, 2003.